Moxie

A HOSPICE CHAPLAIN'S JOURNEY THROUGH GRIEF

CHAPLAIN CANDI WUHRMAN

MOXIE: A Hospice Chaplain's Journey Through Grief

ISBN: 978-1-970157-73-4

Library of Congress Control Number: 1-13663940261

Story Merchant Books
400 S. Burnside Avenue #11B
Los Angeles, CA 90036
www.storymerchantbooks.com

Editing: Charlotte Drummond
Book Interior and E-book Design by Amit Dey (amitdey2528@gmail.com)
Cover Design: Kristina Edstrom & Lexi Mohney
First Printing Edition 2024

TABLE OF CONTENTS

LOVING GUIDANCE

Within *Moxie*, I've included many of my journal entries to demonstrate my processes and engagement through anticipatory, present-day, and past grief to deepen my spiritual connection and open to the greater purpose and value within my relationships.

The experience of grief can be laden with challenging emotions. The writing in this book is an expression of my personal experience. Yours may be different. Please honor your own unique grief journey by seeking the best support that suits you—medical, psychological, and/or spiritual.

The names and relations mentioned are either fictitious or used with permission.

SACRED LANGUAGE

In my work, I use inclusive and inviting language when referring to the Divine because different words, certain names, and particular phrases can hold diverse meanings. Many names can identify and describe a transcendent holy presence.

As a chaplain, I create sacred spaces for each person's unfolding spirituality, advocating for religious and spiritual freedom, and honoring the sanctity of everyone's holy place on this planet. Specific names and words can be inclusive, exclusive, offensive, and even triggering.

Multiple meanings are often associated with sacred terms. I reference names such as Creator, Divine, God, Light, Source, Soul, Spirit, and others as gender neutral. These are not intended to guide you toward a specific belief or theology but serve to articulate a particular emotion, essence, meaning, or value.

Each human being holds a varied set of beliefs. Within my spiritual framework, my Creator and Source of Life has a much broader and greater essence than one particular name. Each may carry an energetic feeling or may emanate a certain quality such as compassion, love, or peace. The ineffable, unexplainable, unseen, intangible, and mysterious may not have a name at all but rather an overall sense of something greater, bigger, or perhaps a higher power. Your spiritual path guides you to the language that resonates within your heart.

In Judaism, the seventy-two names for God express the many facets of a holy presence within our universe. I couldn't possibly name them all. For many Jewish people, God is written with a dash (G-d) in place of the letter O. This custom originates from the biblical text that prohibits erasing God's name or discarding it.

I don't believe one could dispose of God, even in a printed manuscript, and this is not my practice.

I don't mean to be disrespectful to any who follows this custom. My wholehearted intention is to express the Divine's infinite presence. From my perspective, including the letter O expands the divine essence, speaks to the incredible omnipotence of the sacred, and reminds me to remain receptive to life's spiritual lessons and embrace the world wholly.

If you come upon a puzzling thought, pause for a moment to reflect on its interpretation. My sincerest hope is that my language will present possibilities for seeking greater connection, expansion, meaning, and understanding along your spiritual journey.

I will, however, sometimes put a heart in place of the O, to represent G♡d as an open, loving presence.

CALLING IN THE LIGHT

"Calling in the Light" is an invocation that I offer at the beginning of all my individual and group sessions to invite in divine energy and create a sacred space for connection, healing, and transformation. When we invite in a holy presence and divine light, we are opening to awakening to a powerful intervention that elevates our awareness and expands our consciousness.

Divine Source of all Creation, we call ourselves forward into your light and your loving presence. We ask for the clearing of all disease, disharmony, imbalance, negativity, and any fear, worry, and uncertainty that no longer serves us emotionally, mentally, physically, and/or spiritually.

We ask that our Angels, Spirit Guides, and all those who have gone before us be here now. We ask that we be filled, surrounded, and protected with your divine loving energy and radiant Light. We ask for blessings of grace, loving, and compassion for ourselves and others, inner attunement, and alignment to your will and our Divine Highest Self. We ask for divine wisdom, clarity, guidance, understanding, direction, and connection.

As we come together in person or in spirit, we ask for the deepest level of healing, growth, upliftment, release, resolution, liberation, and elevation in consciousness—all for the highest good of all concerned.

Help us remember who we truly are as divine beings having and using our human experiences for our greatest awakening and higher consciousness. We honor the soul's journey and all its curriculum, however that shows up for us. We are grateful for this time together, your presence, and all the healing, transformation, and enlightenment available to us at this time. And so it is.

INTRODUCTION

In the first few months after my mom's death, I was deeply struggling in grief. I felt deep sorrow, numbness, disbelief, and anger, and I wanted to connect with something—anything—different that would hold meaning. For many years, professionals have tried to explain grief in specific stages: denial, anger, bargaining, depression, and acceptance. In my opinion and extensive experience, rather than stages these could be more accurately noted as components of grief, only touching the surface of loss. They are nonlinear, meaning we don't graduate from one level of grief to the next sequentially nor do these components fully address the breadth of the purposeful grief journey. Instead, the array of emotions and experiences leads us on an unorganized and unstructured internal adventure guiding us to search for something meaningful to ground us. These so-called grief stages were originally created as stages of the dying process, still nonlinear, and incorporated some aspects of grief, but my approach is honoring and traveling through the organic path within the whole experience.

When my mom was nearing death, I knew I would begin to grieve but had no clue about what I would need when she died. You see, I am a longtime hospice chaplain with twenty years of experience and have been with thousands of individuals and their entire families as they face end-of-life and the pangs of grief.

Being a Jew and a Jewish Chaplain, I have embraced many Jewish rituals, customs, and traditions such as saying *kaddish*, a prayer honoring life and God that is said during mourning and on the anniversaries of the death of loved ones. In addition, I observed the practice of sitting *shiva*, the seven days following the burial of a dear one, for both my parents after they died. Although these customs are profoundly beautiful, I discovered I needed more. I was not immune to grief, knew it would change my spirit, and that I needed to allow myself to experience this organic journey however it would show up and go wherever it would take me.

Feeling strongly about needing a guide for this journey, I asked a few rabbis in my community if there was a book that could explain and direct me through the spiritual transformation within the grief journey. I needed help finding the purpose of such a grueling experience.

After a few nos along my quest, one rabbi answered me with, "Not that I know of, but if someone wrote it, I'd probably buy it."

I felt something begin to stir inside my belly, something I hadn't felt in a while. Mom always said, "Trust your gut," and I felt it at that moment.

Something began to awaken within me.

Now I believe that at that moment, a bit of moxie energy came alive inside me. I didn't know that I would ultimately do something with that information and hadn't even considered writing a book at that time. But I was struck by a sense of divine inspiration that just might've been channeled through to guide me—and, hopefully, assist you along your grieving journey.

The result is *Moxie: A Hospice Chaplain's Journey Through Grief.* Whatever type of grief you experience, I hope you'll be able to pick this book up at any given time to receive comfort, guidance, inspiration, and solace.

Moxie is somewhat of a personified energy that has become my guide through my grief and beyond. It is a force beyond comprehension and has exceeded all boundaries. You don't have to be afraid of grief as you walk the pebbled healing path. This life force is a divine source that I call moxie, and it's within me and by my side. Your moxie energy may be named differently, but it can also light your way forward.

Chapter 1

WHY MOXIE?

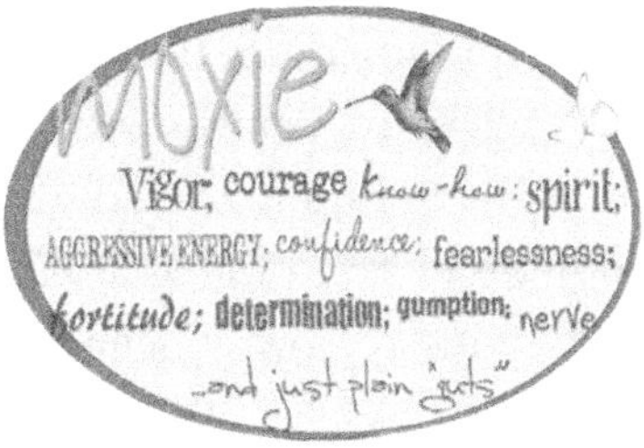

Mom and I played the popular game Scrabble for my entire life, from my childhood until just months before she died. Her fancy Scrabble set was one of the treasures I inherited. Mom taught me about moxie by playing that word in nearly every single game we ever played since I was a little girl.

When it came to games, Mom had no mercy. It was serious business. It completely puzzled me how she picked the letter X every time and repeatedly earned loads of points. I wanted all those points but didn't know the bigger, fancier words. I kept playing anyway.

Growing up, not knowing big swanky words, I thought she was either lucky or really smart. Today, these repetitious lucky streaks have meaning. I wonder now if her formation of the word moxie was a divine message from a higher realm reminding her to align with her vibrant spirit to rise above her tough times.

Each time we played together, I learned more about moxie's meaning. She told me I possessed moxie: a courageous spirit with determination, vigor, verve, and tenacity.

Moxie was one of my mom's favorite words. Spunk was another. Cecile Rose Orenstein Kass Jefferson lived a spunky, courageous, upfront, assertive, incorrigible, feisty, and determined life. She was enthusiastic beyond most folks' comfort and showed her zest for life in just about everything. She'd be off and running with just a spark of your idea sooner than you could even process it. Then, she'd encourage you to dive into the uncharted ponderings of your dreams.

I didn't realize the impact of her enthusiastic energy until she'd died. I spent a good deal of time in my grief journey unpacking its meaning, purpose, and value it might've had throughout my life. I'd be very careful about what I told my mom because I needed to process it first. If I shared something, she'd emotionally and energetically take over with her excitement, or opinion, and I'd get lost. I now realize it was Mom's effort to remain close to me as I was separating from her in the natural part of growing up. I only began to appreciate her later in life.

Unknowingly throughout my life and, with greater awareness, in her death, my mom taught me about strength, resilience, and vibrance—moxie.

Amidst the pain after her death, divine energy propelled me to follow the courageous path of exploring each intricate aspect of grief, seeking every opportunity for spiritual transformation. I inspected the layers of loss and investigated each occurrence to find meaning and purpose as an avenue to rediscover my feisty spirit again, in a new way.

Two months after her passing, I felt the urge to play Scrabble and invited my friend over to play. Looking back, I was seeking comfort in any way possible. Amazed that I even wanted to play a game at that time, I decided to follow the inspiration. Games are important in our family, so it made sense to me.

What happened next completely stunned me: I drew an "X." Was Mom's spirit guiding my hand or was it God? Then I played the word "moxie." I was floored but thrilled and intrigued. *Why now?* After all these years, she wasn't even here to see it. What did this mean for me?

I looked around in shock and shared my amazement with my friend and the significance of this word.

Was Mom here in my living room? It sure felt like it. Was this really happening? Did she help me? I giggled as I felt her energy by my side.

Playing the word "moxie" that night felt like a sign from my mom's spirit. I felt like Mom was telling me she would always be with me, and that she would be able to communicate with me. Being in my home, playing Scrabble, and being comforted by my friend made me realize that something bigger and more powerful was available within my grief. I knew with great certainty that my mom's essence was with me. Sensing her divine spiritual presence gave me such joy and comfort at that moment.

Throughout Mom's life, she followed her instincts even if they didn't conform to the norm. These days, we call that intuition, inspiration, or knowing. She wasn't afraid to share her opinions or compliments.

My husband, Arnie, often called her animated interactions *syrupy*—a little over the top—but I've come to believe her enthusiastic expressions were her amazement and delight with life—all things and all people. When Mom used to visit us in California, Arnie would make her some simple egg salad and Mom would rave about it as the "best egg salad she'd ever had." He felt it was so exaggerated that it bordered on being disingenuous. Egg salad is now a family story of reference. That energy was hard to trust as authentic.

Truthfully, I didn't always feel this affinity toward my mom. As I was developing my personality, there was tension. We faced a lot of challenges over many years. I used to cringe at her enthusiasm, perceiving it as overpowering, and it honestly felt a bit smothering. But she was a colorful, powerful force of nature who made a difference in the world.

For example, my mom would push me toward an opportunity—social or work-related—before I had a chance to process how I felt about it. She may have done this because I was the youngest or she wholeheartedly wanted good things for me, but the result backfired in that it was overwhelming and disempowering giving me the internal message that I couldn't trust my own sense of direction and timing to make my own decisions.

Enthusiasm is similar to excitement but born from a different source. Enthusiasm is defined as eagerness, liveliness, spirit, fervor, and zeal. I only learned later in life that the Latin root of enthusiasm is *entheos*, which is described as "inspired by God." Entheos is sourced from *theo*, the ancient Greek word for God. Enthusiasm is sustainable because it is grounded in divine inspiration, whereas excitement is a response from an outer stimulus.

Moxie is akin to enthusiasm. These are the sparks I believe my mom was attempting to ignite throughout my life, and now, during my grief journey.

My mom's spark would light my way as I further embraced my layers of grief. I became even more keenly aware of the magic and mystery within the revelatory process of feeling, connecting, healing, and changing through pain. These are the tremendous blessings that can manifest within the grief journey.

After years of telling my mom that she would be able to talk to me in some way after she died, this experience felt like a sign that she could communicate with me from the other side. The energy was a palpable, powerful, and bold presence, not unlike my mom's moxie. The Scrabble board moment was simply the inspiration that began to ignite my way and offered me hope, so I could take the next steps through my grief and beyond.

Moxie is our divine spirit coming alive within us. Moxie, this fiery, divine energy, didn't only serve to help me through my grief. It was the fire I needed to awaken my spirit to become the next version of myself and follow the luminous, vibrant energy of the grief journey.

There is something bigger than us that exists universally; within us, around us, and in everything. This energy is empowering.

I'd wanted to connect with my mom's spiritual essence after her death and had been writing to my mom during my morning meditation time. She wasn't talking back to me yet, but I strongly felt her poking at me. I'm pretty sure she was nudging me to write this book. *What is this energy, and why is it here?* I thought.

At the time, these pokes were quite annoying. I wanted to communicate with her, but really, *a book!* I just wanted a simple conversation—or even a word—that indicated she was with me. Although I'd begun writing other books, I never considered that writing a book could assist me on my grief journey as well as help to guide others through loss, too.

I questioned myself. *Do I really have a message to share? Are my thoughts even clear enough amidst this pain to write anything?* I was feeling pretty low.

Suddenly, I heard my mom saying, "Get off of it, Candi. Just do it. You can do this. We can do this. Go for it," with so much excitement, enthusiasm, and zeal—moxie? Oy! I'm certain that the initiation of this messaging at this point was my mom saying, "This is your moxie, grab hold of it."

This jolt was completely annoying! But it also woke me up.

Some powerful force was trying to get my attention, but my inner fire wasn't strong enough yet. I was hurting; nothing felt right. Physical and emotional exhaustion were the norms of the day. I experienced constant uncertainty about each next move and whether it was the right one.

Real and very raw emotions, although necessary, were bubbling over in all my activities and relationships. My nerves were sensitive and on edge. I felt insecure about most things. Interests in life as I knew them had flattened, and I was just taking one step at a time, searching for a sense of comfort, connection, grounding, and understanding.

Shock does not begin to describe my feelings when presented with the idea of writing this book. I had never considered myself a writer, and although I own many books, I was not a big reader throughout my life. Yet one thing led to another, and here I am. As I was writing, divine guidance nudged me to take the next step and write more. Maybe my experience could help others facing the same reality.

An experience, a phone call, a text, a movie, a book, or an encounter continued showing up on this writing journey, which affirmed and reaffirmed that this was the right track. Sometimes, I would read an inspirational card, initiate a spirit-to-spirit dialogue with my mom, see a hummingbird (which is a sign from my mom's spirit), have a thought, or I would get the divine "hit" that the universal energies were lining up in just the right way.

Inside of myself, I felt strong messages.

"Keep listening and trust your inspiration, instincts, and intuition."

"Answer the call."

"Follow your energy."

"Feel and connect."

"Say no to what doesn't serve you."

"Say yes to yourself, your spirit, your light, and your divine energy."

I read Elizabeth Gilbert's book, *Big Magic*, a compilation of stories about how our creative energy awakens and guides us to particular callings and endeavors. With new awareness, we get to choose if we will accept the opportunity to engage with a new vibrant adventure to explore and grow our spirit. I felt supported and encouraged to follow my magic and trust the mysterious ways that *moxie* was showing up for me.

Spirit can whisper and swirl through us. If we pay attention and embrace divine moments of inspiration, the sacred source of our life can enlighten and enliven us.

Chapter 2

SAYING YES TO THE UNIVERSE

"Things happen that guide us in particularly perfect directions for our deep healing and profound transformation."

–Chaplain Candi Wuhrman

Early in this writing process, I accepted two speaking engagements. I had an inkling that these invitations would perfectly support my book-writing journey, but I had no idea of their full impact at the time. Each of these engagements was scheduled months in advance and arrived at the perfect moment to fuel and inspire the next segment of this book.

The first audience, Women in Spirituality, was made up of female group members who engage in learning opportunities involving different religious and spiritual beliefs and practices.

The women's group enjoyed my first presentation about Jewish spirituality, knew of my work in the field of death, dying, grief, and loss, and requested a follow-up engagement to explore the spiritual transformation that comes through grief.

The date of the talk was auspiciously scheduled on the anniversary of my mom's death, which was delightfully unexpected. Alignments such as this are always divinely intriguing.

Universal spiritual energy seems to align synchronicities beautifully.

On the day of the presentation, I felt thrilled to be honoring my mom's memory, blessing the women, deepening connections, and encouraging spiritual growth. Sharing the richness of Jewish traditions, facilitating harmonious multifaith conversation and learning, alleviating fears around death, and nurturing grief healing all contributed to making my mom's memory a blessing.

The second invitation, which had also been scheduled months ahead, was for an interview on Transformation Talk Radio with my friend and colleague Susan Dolci on the transformational experiences of death, dying, grief, and loss. This engagement had been arranged serendipitously on the day before my mom's birthday, and I believe these were not random coincidences but rather divine appointments that I consider profoundly sacred, and I accept them with appreciation and gratitude.

The radio talk was titled "From Devastation to Fulfillment: The Spiritual Transformation of Grief," and by the time I appeared on the show, Susan had already read the first pages of my book in their raw and unedited form, which invigorated our discussion.

During the interview, I described my devastating unraveling in grief when I called out to my mom after she died, saying, "Mama, are you there?"

When I couldn't sense my mom's presence anywhere in my energetic field, I called out verbally and then in writing to my dad, who had died twenty-six years earlier and to whom I had only spoken to once in the spiritual realm since his death, and I asked, "Dad, have you seen Mom? Is she okay?"

In my journal, my dad responded by letting me know she was okay but had a lot to do there for a while. This gave me great comfort. Although I'd not been particularly drawn to reach out to my dad in this way in the past, I was grateful for his forthcoming response.

Journal writing is an effective tool for expressing emotions and traveling the inner energetic experience of a surfacing issue. I use writing to reach out and connect with my deceased loved ones and open the space for them to communicate back with me. This is a possible aspect of mediumship where one can connect with a person's spiritual essence, but one does not have to be a medium to be aware of the presence of a loved one's spirit.

The Women in Spirituality group asked me to return yet again to speak on "Befriending Death," and I responded with a resounding "Yes!"

Not only do I love speaking, but I also find joy in talking about death and dying and easing the universal discomfort around the anticipation and uncertainty of the dying process. Profound engagement and connection are possible when families share anticipatory grief, underlying fears, old wounds, and heartfelt hopes and dreams with each other. They even share humor as they ponder the unusual and mysterious ways a loved one's spirit may show up after death.

The end is never the end; it is undeniably a new beginning. Grief is the most complex, confusing, and misunderstood experience. With a human death, a life ends, but at the same time, another part of life's journey begins. This is the circle of life. It's like shedding an old skin and reemerging anew. Grief and the experience of loss change us. We each accept the journey in different ways. In my grief, I wrote a book that illuminates and illustrates the multiple components of the unraveling, unfolding, immersing, healing, recalibrating, and loving that I experienced through my loss journey. For others, it could be an art project or another type of transformational pathway.

In my chaplaincy, counseling, and coaching services, I guide individuals and families through this exploratory and revelatory transformational process. Being resourceful is finding the people, places, and programs that support you in connecting with the aligned inner path that's right for you to make your grief journey the most fulfilling, nourishing, and satisfying.

Feel free to glance at the end of the book in the section called "Being ReSourceful" for more information about this.

My spirit kept guiding me to carry forward with moxie. In a spiritual context, every occurrence offers a divine perspective. Business lulls, health shifts, and body stressors nudge us to expand our energies again and again.

My dad and my stepmom, Lynda, loved to sail. I remember Dad saying something similar to this quote by Jackson Brown, Jr.: "If you can't change the direction of the wind, simply adjust your sail."

Inner conflict is often the wind beneath our wings. My grief and my inner turmoil caused me to seek Spirit and ask for direction. And that, in conjunction with my mom, led me to complete this book. Amidst my fears, doubts, and tears, I considered throwing in the towel but immediately heard my mom seemingly whisper in my ear, "Get on with it, Candi."

Initially, I heard those words with impatience as in my younger days, but the energy quickly shifted to an internal confidence-boosting message: "Because you can."

At this moment, the proverbial fork in the road presented my options. One was to allow the difficulty to hold me back. The other was to call on my moxie energy to propel me forward. Well, you can see which road I chose.

I am profoundly aware of the continuation of all—our exploration, healing, grief, growth, life struggles—our learning and transformation about all the workings of a lifetime.

More importantly, through life's journey, the awakening to something greater always comes with magic, mystery, and a Spiritful adventure.

Grief is a messy journey filled with multiple layers of emotions that we think will last forever. We don't need to fear big emotions and mountains of uncertainty, because there is great purpose in it all. As you read this book, you will find there is great transformation and understanding available within the grief experience.

This nudging, pushing, calling, and urging was real and palpable. Was it Mom or was it God? I wasn't quite sure. It was a surge of energy that was alive, an enthusiasm and drive that felt purposeful and bigger than, and beyond, me.

Along my grief journey, random signs generated thoughts of my mom. Sparks of my mom's light made me aware of her energy and stirred the reemergence of my moxie to encourage me to move forward. She was the burning lamp lighting my way. Receiving these awakenings amidst my painful grief, I came to understand these instances as love notes from my mom and guidance from the Divine, giving me direction, reassurance, and the strength to carry on.

Moxie illustrates my journey with my mom as she aged, changed, declined, and died. Many conversations embraced her contemplation about aging, changing, death, and beyond. As I recognized my mom's spiritual energy following her death and discovered her attempts to talk to me with clever flashes of insight through my grief, I was engaging her vibrant moxie and keeping her memory alive.

These fascinating serendipitous moments where I felt Mom's presence after her death reaffirmed for me that communication with our deceased loved ones does exist. When my dad died nearly thirty years earlier, I only had just begun to deepen my spirituality, and over time, I became more aware of his spiritual essence nearby at times. These encounters reassured me that their spirits would always be with me in deep tangible ways.

Knowing these sacred connections were possible and having experienced similar occurrences throughout the years following my dad's death deepened my grief experience with my mom. Her continued presence brought tremendous comfort and awakened me to her deep unending love. Her spirit inspires me to embrace my authenticity with audacity. When our loved ones die, they pass a torch of light to each of us, bringing opportunities to awaken our inner spirit, propel us forward, revitalize a dream, and encourage us to contribute in more fulfilling ways.

An illuminated path is tough to see when the pain is so great. Many people recoil at the very thought of grieving a loss, but the experience of grief is purposeful. Grief is a nonlinear journey of unraveling, unpacking, and unfolding the life events and memories of a person's impact on our lives and our hearts. Within that journey, doors and windows open to a variety of avenues for discovery; healing from our younger years and the layers of relationship encounters that are recorded within our psyche and spirit. This is why grief is so complicated, crazy-making, and daunting.

My grief has been the impetus that prompted my desire to bring more comfort and understanding to the puzzling experiences of an aging parent, a declining loved one, and the turmoil and devastation of loss.

None of us are immune to grief and loss. If we care about, like, or love someone at all, we will grieve. As I embrace the pain of loss and further awaken my spirit, I share vulnerable revelations within my relationships and reveal the purpose, value, and enlightenment that come from going through the anguish and heartache of a loved one's physical absence.

With better understanding and by discovering impactful points within our experiences, we can navigate the bumpy landscape of death and dying with greater grace, peace, and even joy. By accepting the opportunities for growth and transformation put before us, we are saying yes to a life bigger than we could ever imagine.

Chapter 3

UNDAUNTING COURAGE

"Unraveling…is letting go in the best possible way…
untangling the knots that hold you back…unwrapping
the gifts you've hidden for too long…the potential
that's always been there…ditching the labels and
the should-haves and letting yourself be
what you were always meant to be."

—Susannah Conway

On a very still and quiet afternoon, about four months after my mom died, one of my hospice patients introduced me to her favorite book, *Undaunted Courage* by Stephen Ambrose. I'd never heard of it at the time. She made me promise to read it.

In full transparency, I haven't read it yet, but the title resonated deeply and made an imprint on my soul. I repeatedly referred to this title as *undaunting* versus undaunted until a coworker ever-so-graciously corrected me.

The message that came through was that one of my goals in life had been to have undaunting courage—to live life fearlessly without a shred of intimidation in all situations. We can have fearless moments and feel secure in many situations but not all. So, what might this mean? How might this powerful phrase fuel our souls?

Undaunting fits with my belief that life is an active journey rather than a passive one—an ongoing engaging energy calling to our courageous spirit. This is moxie being employed at every opportunity.

This patient—feisty, strong-willed, and committed to her life's journey—was aware that she was dying and thought she was ready. However, she was ticked off when her departure was not according to her time frame which prompted a more extensive life review. We never know the exact divine timing of the end of our lives. For this patient, as for many on hospice, this frustration nudged her to explore her life a bit more deeply.

She was a loving, attentive mom, a proud veteran, and an avid sports fan. Interestingly, she was close to my mom's age and possessed a similar zest for life. She presented as though she'd conquered a multitude of challenges throughout her life. Sitting with this patient and listening to stories as she contemplated her life, I was deeply touched that she viewed life's adversities and uncertainties as astounding adventures that illuminated her profound courage and strength—a divine message that I needed for comfort in my own daunting place while immersed in my grief without my mom. I also sensed her adult children might need to hear it following her death to transmit her courage, faith, and strength for their own life experiences.

I wrote this poem first for myself to clarify and articulate my deeper process of the challenges with grief and then for my patient's family because it illustrated the value of deep contemplation on the meaning of life's lessons we face in the transformation through grief.

Undaunting Courage.
What does that mean?
Going forward regardless because you're called to do so.

Fearlessly? Quite the contrary!
Feeling the fear, apprehension, and unknown,
and charging forward anyway.
Slaying the dragons at your feet and being grateful
they're not at your head.
Becoming the hero in your own journey rather
than comparing yours to another.
Hearing the wisdom in your heart and living it.
Trusting God and the Universe even when you
hit some bumpy roads.
Undaunting Courage.
Taking each day as it comes, whatever life brings,
and creating the most
Miraculous victory for yourself and others with
dignity, grace, and compassion.

My patient trusted her life's journey had been exactly what it was supposed to be. She kept leaning into whatever was in front of her and what brought her joy as well as her faith, but not without unknowns. So, as she reflected on the travels in *Undaunted Courage,* I asked how she aligned her life with this story. She shared her awareness of her life's mysterious twists and turns of adventure and acknowledged her strength, courage, and boldness—*moxie*—with each step.

Chaplaincy, and specifically Hospice Chaplaincy, is a unique calling. It's not just a job. It literally chose me. In this multidimensional role, I work with the patient's narrative to connect the meaningful, purposeful, and valuable experiences within their life's tapestry. I'm serving the patient and their family as they process their lives—providing solace and direction. All of these levels of engagement are happening simultaneously. My job is to weave it all together. Throughout the end-of-life period, each patient and their loved ones are facing their relationship successes and failures. As one's stories are shared, life's difficulties and heroic acts are revealed. Reviewing a patient's life narrative exemplifies their impact on the world. With deep contemplation, we discover what lessons we need through our grief and healing. These chaplaincy assignments involving multiple engagements and conversations inspire my own personal spiritual growth and learning as well.

Hospice work, in general, is a calling. You know what a calling is—the energy that pulls on you while being an integral part of you, throughout your entire body, in your bones, at every turn. You can't shake it. It's relentless. The sensations may even be uncomfortable because the call is an invitation from a higher, divine place. When these messages come, they cannot be denied for long.

I had experienced a couple of deaths earlier in my life, but when my stepfather died and I was by his side, I felt something different and unique, became intrigued, and realized there was something bigger and beyond physical comprehension that was occurring. Immersing myself in end-of-life and grief work allows me to live in the unexplainable, mysterious, and unpredictable, and gives me the great joy and satisfaction of helping individuals and families discover the profoundly sacred experience of life and death.

This energy has a purpose. Whenever and wherever we are called, it's a good idea to answer the tone, attune to the request, and accept the appointment. The guidance and direction are not always simple, but the rewards are great when we persevere.

After my mom's death, finding my moxie again required a high degree of undaunting courage and tenacity. As I connect to my inner spirit, I have reflected on the many age stages and layers of mother-daughter experiences that affected my life. I developed greater trust that the pain of revisiting the memories and the messages received from my mom throughout my years held deeper meaning, purpose, and value.

My mom was certain that my feisty spirit would change the world but was often far more excited about it than I was. Sure, I was excited and enthused about various opportunities, but my drive and determination didn't seem to match hers regarding my life choices. My mom and I were quite similar; both emotional and excitable, interested in what makes a person tick, human relationships, a faith in humanity, and optimism about life. However, Mom would often put the cart before the horse. She'd be excited about what she thought was a good idea but didn't have the patience to allow someone to come around to the benefits of an idea in their own time. It felt a bit overbearing. I think her intention was to instill interest and foster motivation. She'd conquered many of her fears over certain endeavors. However, she overlooked that we each need to embrace life's opportunities as they call to and resonate within us. The challenges and cringes that occurred when I felt pushed and pulled to something she desired became the impetus for learning to empower myself and trust how my inner spirit was being called...Even when it didn't fit her ideal for me. The spiritual journey is not for the faint of heart. So, why do I keep going? The answer is that it is too painful to stay where I am. I must keep moving forward. I cannot go back to sleep. Yes, I said sleep. Spiritual transformation is about awakening.

We are not talking about a religious experience necessarily, although you may have some references that relate to a religious practice or belief. Moreover, I am speaking of the adventures that enliven the human spirit—the soul awakening. That might mean your own burning bush or Mount Sinai revelation, or it could mean the enlightening of the heart—one twinge, pinch, tingle, or nudge at a time—that guides you from one steppingstone to another.

Waking up parts of ourselves where we deeply connect and listen to the stirring within the soul can bring emotional, mental, and physical discomfort and then, immense joy.

I am a feeler. I feel everything. I feel my emotions deeply and express them—particularly the depth of sadness with loss. When a wave comes over me, I truly need to be immersed in it to really grasp its meaning. When I'm in a deep process, I embrace it and follow its emotional energy to see what it's telling and teaching me. I seek the resolution of that particular issue. I feel sensations in all parts of my body, and I ask that part what message it has for me and travel with my body's energy to complete the process. This active process could take minutes or days to resolve a specific experience. This has been my practice for over three decades well before it was given a name—Internal Family Systems (IFS) and became a methodology that encouraged having a relationship with these different parts of ourselves. We all have the ability to feel deeply, but many of us only feel from the neck up, which means we try to think about what we feel, cut off its flow, and minimize the value of the emotional experience. We are all energetic beings living by Divine life support as our Source blows breath into us every second.

Our Creator is giving us life with every breath. Each person is more accurately described as a spiritual being engaging in a multitude of human encounters each day. We are souls in divine partnership with the physical body.

An array of emotions and energetic awakening can be perceived as negative or positive, good or bad, pleasant or terrifying, with pain and sorrow. When a beautiful awareness arises, joyful elation and great enthusiasm can also come rushing in. All of which can be overwhelming. I know from years of working in the field of spirituality, awakening, and transformation that big inner experience leads to a profound connection to one's inner spirit and even greater outer contributions to the betterment of society.

Given that everything is energy, feeling the intense sensations that are often accompanied by big emotions is challenging for most of us. Sometimes, the waves of emotions and a rush of energy throughout our bodies can hit us like a tsunami.

I've never experienced a tsunami; however,
I can only imagine that kind of turmoil would be
intense terror that would never end.

With the intensity of profound awakenings, the waves of my emotions have been very powerful, all-consuming, and persistent. When these surges of emotions and energy initially began, I felt very odd and didn't know quite how to manage the floodgates. Early on in my life, I shut down my emotions because I felt a lot of pain, so I learned to cope with food and alcohol. Numbness was better than pain, sorrow, and confusion. When the channels opened, I felt quite alone and a mess. I didn't know that these big emotions were ok. The flooding of feelings felt utterly overwhelming, uncontrollable, and unmanageable. I felt afraid. Each time these waves came in, I'd tighten up and brace myself for the unpredictable period of these unexplainable expressions of hurt, sadness, and a loss of hope. No one I knew had ever shown me how to be with myself in these deep cathartic expressions. Sometimes I cried loudly, big tears, huge sobs. Some people call this ugly crying, but I don't think it's ugly at all. I think of a precious child sobbing heavily without understanding just fully feeling every facet of the experience. There was no rationale. My expression of emotions wasn't always understandable to someone witnessing them, but I was grateful when someone sat with me and made space for the unexplainable.

Even years after learning how to express my feelings, I've experienced professionals—other chaplains, therapists, and social workers—uncomfortable witnessing big emotions. It becomes quite clear very quickly who has allowed themselves to deeply experience raw emotions and who feels a strong urge to curtail and contain a person's full expression. An important note: You'll want to choose a professional who does their own deep, fully embodied expressive inner transformational work…and engages in healing modalities and practices in their regular routine.

Being in touch with my feelings and the energetic force within my soul and body is my superpower. I attune to my own heart and soul experience, as well as that of others. I am deeply connected with both the finite earth and the infinite heavenly realms. However, I am intensely mindful of how these vast feelings can be tremendously uncomfortable. My whole body becomes awakened, and this is how I know what is true, how I transform, and how I connect with the greatest part of myself—my soul.

I keep going because this is the way I keep coming back to myself, again and again.

My acronym for SELF—the Higher Self—is Source Energy Loving Force. Our Source resides within us, and it is our greatest energetic reservoir of love and is an undeniable force that we must embrace.

One day, as I dove into my meditation and self-reflective time, I had to confront my fear. In my rigorously honest self-examination, I discovered that I cannot with full integrity speak about stepping into my moxie without talking about fear.

To my recollection, no one in my family ever shared their fear with me. I didn't know it was a normal emotion. I don't know that anyone ever told me not to be afraid directly, but yet minimized my fear by telling me there was nothing to fear in a given situation. I thought it was the plague and a true defect of character. Even after many years of addiction recovery, therapy, spiritual healing, and inner transformation, I still felt a lot of shame about being afraid. It was like a dirty little secret. The message I received growing up was that we are supposed to charge forward in life fearlessly. Or at least act like we're not afraid: feel the fear and do it anyway.

While charging forward despite fear can be successful, I'm also keenly aware that the energy of fear can guide my growth and healing for my life journey. This process of self-discovery presents valuable revelations for my spiritual transformation that empowers me to step into a new garment, a stronger skin, and awakens me to an awe-inspiring life. The transformational power that ignites me by walking "through the valley of the shadow of death" repeatedly illuminates my path and fuels my spirit.

Fear is not something I ever want to admit or talk about. I would rather avoid it, wish that enough faith would drown it out, and yet, it is my constant companion. *Oy vey! Enough already.*

I wanted to give up and run away, but at the same time, I felt loyal to completing this heartfelt writing journey. However, my energy was heavy, and I felt a sense of drudgery within my gut. *What now?* This writing was taking longer than I had hoped. To use a marathon phrase,

I hit a wall. Several of my circles knew of my commitment to the project. I had even promised a few signed copies after its publication. The power within me was too strong to turn back now. This was the challenge of deciding to come out of hiding and be bold.

The beginning of one of my favorite quotes is by Marianne Williamson, from her book, *A Return to Love: Reflections on the Principles of A Course in Miracles:* "Our deepest fear is not that we are inadequate. Our deepest fear is that we are powerful beyond measure. It is our light, not our darkness, that most frightens us." I adore the entire quote and have read it often over the years. As this writing process challenged me to face my deepest fear, I want to share one inner dialogue exercise that surfaced as I wrestled with this aspect of myself:

> *Candi:* Fear, what are you about today? Would you speak, please?
>
> *Fear:* Yes, I am fear. I am throughout your whole being. I am here to teach you. You don't need to run from me, from your body; you need to feel my energy to conquer and befriend me.
>
> *Candi:* What do you want me to know, and why is your energy so uncomfortable?
>
> *Fear:* I am actually a powerful force within you. Remember the FEAR acronyms: Face Everything And Respond or Feel [and] Embrace [your] Authentic Reality.
>
> *Candi:* Yes, and…
>
> *Fear:* There is great power here. You have felt discomfort because it is a great surge that is permeating your body that is coming through your pores. Remember what you told your children, Michelle and Josh, when you were taking them to summer sleepaway camp years ago? Excitement is the same line of energy as fear.
>
> *Candi:* Yes, but how do I integrate this powerful energy?

Fear: You have to get into your body and use your energy… your bike, walking in the trees, yoga, workouts. Just keep walking forward and keep writing.

Candi: Oh, I feel my stomach acting jumpy. I don't want to move. I want to write more about it now. I need to move and only have so much time.

Fear: Yes. Be still and connect inside. Get clear on the one thing that will be good for your body, mind, and spirit, and then, do that. Trust that clarity.

What popped into my consciousness immediately was to move my body and make a phone call to a friend. In addition to prayer, meditation, and these inner dialogues, making phone calls to connect with others helps me know that I am not alone in my fearful moments and that connectedness diminishes their intensity. This powerful energy is purposeful.

The most amazing part is that making the phone call showed me the divine hand in the whole journey. My friend shared her fears about moving forward with her creativity. Hearing her openness, invitation, and vulnerability to engage permitted me to share my angst and apprehension. The connection I felt in that one phone call gave me great comfort that I was on this unfolding journey with another human and that it was safe to be authentic and transparent. Connecting deeply with another soul left me awestruck, which helped me better understand myself and further expand the feeling of Divine Presence all around me. It felt like there was something bigger at play here making my expanding world more inviting rather than terrifying. As I walked among the gorgeous Oregon trees, I felt the great expanse and the nourishment of the sunshine. These experiences left me wondering if we have these giant emotions to connect with others out of need. We can move through fear and thrive in support of one another.

When I first felt this fearful energy, I felt stirrings in my heart. Then the sensations quickly moved to my gut. Knowing that shame is often felt in the belly, I sat with and clarified that it was indeed the energy of shame. The flutterings in my body were traveling down through my legs, my thighs, my shins, and my calves.

I asked these new feelings, "What messages do you have for me?" Often, the emotions we feel have a voice to express that can reveal a deeper meaning, leading us to our greater healing for that time. I was specifically interested in this inner journey revealing the transformational opportunities that would resolve the current struggles within this phase of my writing.

The energy that surfaced was fear, plain and simple, at its core. However, the beliefs that were underneath the fear were shameful messages questioning if I was capable enough, sharp enough, and smart enough.

In Judaism, the Hebrew word *yirah* is defined as both "fear" and "awe." How could that be?

You may have heard the phrase "the fear of God." I had to unpack that one for myself as well. Why would I want a God in my life that I feared? It felt very uncomfortable, unpleasant, and initially punitive because that is how I thought of fear. This premise is about respecting the magnitude and vastness of God.

What I have discovered in *yirah* is that becoming aware of the awe-inspiring, awe-some, awe-struck power of Divine presence and the energy within us and all around us is bigger than I could ever imagine. We can call that energy many different names or no name at all.

The relationship to the Divine is a series of individual ever-evolving, unfolding experiences. We always have a choice to determine what fits for each one of us. That choice is not to be taken lightly. We need to trust that the energy of fear and the feelings of awe have great purpose and value and are calling us to listen deeply.

For me to truly embody the quality and energy of moxie—courage, boldness, and a vibrant fiery spirit—I must place all my cards on the table, and as my dad always told me, "You gotta play the hand you're dealt."

I had great parents, but as with all humans, they had their faults, difficulties, and challenges.

Growing up in the sixties and at the time that my parents divorced, the available resources were limited, and I struggled. I absorbed energies that were not acknowledged because my parents followed their parents' examples. They learned that if something was unpleasant or unbecoming, they needed to push it down, pack it away, and then find their strength and determination.

That is moxie, too, right?

Absolutely, and there is a significant difference between willing something to be different—mind over matter—and acknowledging the difficulty and seeking to heal its origin to walk freely and authentically. The first, mind over matter or wanting something to be different, is like *The Little Engine That Could*, which holds the implication that we should draw on our inner inspiration and formulate a strong self-belief.

However, this exertion of willpower can be a spiritual bypass. This determination attempts to overpower the inner doubt and fear and squelch its energy. These efforts require a huge amount of our energy. We have the power to do this for a while. However, in my experience, it cannot be sustainable long term. The experience becomes increasingly more difficult and is much like swimming upstream against the current with great resistance to the natural flow of the river of life.

Diving into the origin of fear is something entirely different. The body does not lie. It knows the truth. We are energetic beings. Connecting with the energies running through the body allows us to reveal the true stories of our history.

Many of you may be saying, "But that story is way too painful, I would rather not go there." I have heard this statement many times. We have to first accept ourselves exactly where we are at any given moment.

For me, I must go there. I cannot deny the call for healing and transformation. I cannot hold what feels like a secret. The pain of holding back becomes too painful. My moxie is deciding to tell my truth courageously and boldly, with great conviction, in the hope that hearing and seeing my experience will propel others into greater healing, deeper connection, and the freedom to transform into their most brilliant, authentic self.

These next pieces of information are crucial in deciphering intergenerational, inherited energetic patterns.

I will dive more deeply into intergenerational, inherited family patterns later in the book. For this initial process of moving forward in the face of the unknown, I'll explain this awareness more simply for now.

The brief explanation of how intergenerational patterns are transmitted is by someone having emotions such as fear and shame and not owning them. In other words, if our parents were afraid, attempted to bury or deny the fear's existence, the energy is still prevalent. The child feels the parent's fearful energy, but the words spoken by the parent and their energetic presence do not match. This parent-child exchange produces confusion and a sense of incongruence. Children are very perceptive and know what they know by what they feel.

I felt a very strong sense that one source of this fearful energy belonged to my mom, and by mere exposure, I absorbed it and took it on as my own. My mom never acted like she was afraid, but she was. Her actions didn't match the energy I felt.

I have two older sisters. She may have shared it with them but not with me. I'm guessing she didn't share with me because she wanted me to think she was strong.

In my early teens, I remember my mom telling me I was perceptive and sharp after sharing something I read. She acknowledged these qualities in me. That's the only time I remember hearing this praise. Although the nice compliments felt good, I now see that at that time in her life, she felt better about herself, was in a stable marriage, and was more adjusted and confident. I suppose she felt more in control and more able to acknowledge these qualities in me. It is fascinating and confusing that the words *capable*, *sharp*, and *smart* surfaced because I think these may have been the very qualities Mom wanted to possess at the time of her divorce from my dad.

For the sake of sharing some of my unconventional healing modalities in print, let's jump into a spirit-to-spirit dialogue with Mom and get a little clarity on my fear awareness. I'll be interjecting spirit-to-spirit conversations with my mom and dad in various places throughout the book. They are a way to receive confirmation and clarity within a situation as well as a means for a beautiful ongoing relationship with my deceased parents. Processing in this type of dialogue is a very powerful mechanism for walking through the fear and deep emotions of uncertainty when those feelings arise.

Candi: Hey Mom, I need to get some clarity on this fear thing. You never talked about your fear, and we never discussed it before you died. I am sure you were afraid because you were human, and human beings feel fear. It's something I have been plagued with throughout my life. I feel like I absorbed a lot of that energy from you. I knew I would have fears of my own. However, I don't think I should be plagued with this energy. What can you tell me about fear, keeping feelings secret, and what you know now?

> *Mom:* I am so glad you're bringing this forward. I know it is hard to talk about because we buried, or at least we thought we buried, our fears. We thought we were supposed to keep fighting it, and if we didn't acknowledge it, we could believe it didn't exist. We thought we were supposed to be in control, all-powerful, and run over those deficits—at least, we thought they were deficits. I can see how you picked up that energy. I don't entirely understand it. I now get that you felt there was something hidden. We didn't know about energy then. I am very sorry that we didn't know. We just didn't. But you do now. I know you feel all of this in your body. Let your body be your guide. Listen to your feelings. I know we have been ridiculed for our emotions. Move beyond that and be emotionally honest. Use your autonomy now to assist in greater transformation and connection.

I had to trust that there was a better way to do life. I opened up to something bigger and unknown. The work was on myself and brought about my transformation as I sought to understand a Divine Source—something bigger than myself.

Each of my moments of spiritual awakening has awakened me to something greater; the sacred and holy presence of the unseen, intangible, unexplainable force that is beyond my comprehension, and that keeps me coming back to myself. The awe is standing taller within my divine power—my moxie—bringing it all to the table and embracing the whole of who I am...divine and human experiencing both fear and awe.

I feel fear when I share wholeheartedly about God. Growing up Jewish in the South, sometimes referred to as the Bible Belt, I created pat answers for who and what I believed about Jesus for my own preservation. The Ku Klux Klan, evangelism, and proselytizing were prevalent in that time, and unfortunately still are today. I only lived the first three years of my life in Mississippi, but in that short time energetically absorbed the fear of living freely with my full identity. I suspect this occurred within my home and our community. My awareness is that fearful and anxious energies are transmitted to others and taken on when fear is present, not acknowledged nor addressed, and then hinders the freedom of the human spirit. This is one of the many ways our voices, emotions, and inner spirits have been suppressed.

In the field of chaplaincy, we advocate for religious and spiritual freedom. Everyone has the divine right to believe in and see their Creator in whatever way resonates with each of them. This fear and apprehension of sharing my true beliefs has stayed with me and created internal conflict about truly expressing my love for God. Having a fear of expressing my love and admiration for my Divine Creator made me afraid that I might seem evangelical and proselytizing.

Even as I write this today, I feel terror in my heart from the belief that it wasn't safe to express my true feelings. I cannot sidestep these feelings any longer.

Acknowledging these fears ignites my moxie energy. Evangelism and proselytizing communicate a message that one should believe in only one way—that way—and don't allow for an individual to freely open to a personal experience of Divine Presence. Speaking my true beliefs and standing up for what I believe—the freedom to discover and live one's own beliefs—releases the block of fear that has covered my heart.

I am now able to fully inhale the energy of God. To feel the awe of God, we must embark on an unknown journey through the arid desert into our sweet, promised land—the source of divine energy that runs in and through our entire mind, body, and spirit.

For this very reason, fear and awe are in tandem. We must engage our fear to embrace our moxie. Courage is not the absence of fear but the willingness to walk forward despite it, with the deep knowing that we will be stronger and braver for accepting the tasks before us. The fulfillment of our promised land is tapping into our vibrant moxie, which offers us opportunities to stand taller with boundless purpose and a sense of contributing valuably to the world and all of humanity.

Diving deeply inside myself to find my moxie to write this book, in and of itself, has been a transformational journey. The inner turmoil has been excruciating. The grief changes from being all about the loss of my mom and missing her physical presence to engaging in my entire spirit's recalibration without her and awakening into bolder versions of myself. The process has been challenging and liberating. This transformational process encompasses the experiences of becoming who I am, owning my gifts, being seen, and standing in my God-given strength and power. The journey is terrifying and enlightening and calls for tremendous courage and strength of heart.

Writing about this process gives me greater clarity. Grief and spiritual energetic shifts can cause physical reactions. Without being too descriptive, my body has experienced upheavals galore with reactions from my head to my toes. I have experienced highs and lows, distraction and presence, excitement and depression, inspiration and doubt, and resistance and enthusiasm. Discovering, rediscovering, and reigniting my moxie has been challenging work, especially when I didn't know that was what was happening.

Loss is very real. The inner void creates a vacuum. One might call that vast cavern of emptiness a dark hole. I suppose it could have multiple names. In that internal space that had once experienced inner fulfillment, either from the profound connection with another person or within one's profession, an absence is experienced. That void offers a stillness that speaks to us. It's a space to befriend. We could call that a divine and sacred space of awakening. When we listen in the stillness and quiet hollow opening, that space becomes a hallowed place.

My choice is to dive deeply into my inner process in response to an internal desire to heal my spirit. My still small inner voice summons me to courageously travel deep within my soul. It is attuning to a deeper listening to Source Energy awakening another path for me. This voice is not audible like you and I might hear one another but hearing a word or phrase somewhere in your body. When I first began to attune to my internal experience, I'd get an inner feeling to turn right down a street, call a particular person, and just a couple of words like, "trust me." Over the years, and yearning for others to share this experience, I am keenly aware and acknowledge that this is my path, and it may not suit everyone.

The desire to grow beyond, rise above, and create greater meaning from my difficulties by honoring my inner call became stronger than remaining stagnant and in pain. Judaism teaches us to live beyond a mediocre life and engage in life fully. Finding meaning and purpose in the discomfort and turmoil inside my body and soul was leading me through a sacred recalibration and transformation. Opportunities were being presented to use my mom's life, our relationship, the death and dying process, and my grief experience for blessings in healing service to others.

Marianne Williamson's quote is worthy of noting in its entirety now:

"Our deepest fear is not that we are inadequate.
Our deepest fear is that we are powerful beyond measure.
It is our light, not our darkness, that most frightens us.
We ask ourselves, Who am I to be brilliant, gorgeous, talented, fabulous?
Actually, who are you not to be?
You are a child of God.
Your playing small does not serve the world.
There's nothing enlightened about shrinking so that other people won't feel insecure around you.
We are all meant to shine, as children do.
We were born to make manifest the glory of God that is within us.
It's not just in some of us; it's in everyone.
And as we let our own light shine, we unconsciously give other people permission to do the same.
As we're liberated from our own fear, our presence automatically liberates others."

These words led me through a great deal of fear and helped me recognize my Divine Light, and that I possess God-given gifts to share with the world. Drawing on the glory of God from the depth of our soul, we are called to live boldly, courageously, and vibrantly. Understanding our God-given truth and gifts bestowed upon us takes a lifetime. We become aware and step forward by ongoing achievable actions—steppingstones—which are the pathway to our gifts.

In Judaism, we speak of the Neshama, the soul, and often refer to it as the lamp of God, our Divine Light that resides within us. That Divine essence is embedded in every fiber of our being. The soul is immortal. Our bodies resemble a strong, vibrant candle with a heavenly fire that dances brilliantly. From Psalm 18: "For You light my lamp, Hashem, My God brightens my darkness."

Owning that Divine essence is the challenging part. Some days, I know it and feel it. Other days, I don't. Why is that? My daily spiritual practices offer me a path to process my inner turmoil, which then clears the path for divine light to shine. Engaging in a regular spiritual attunement practice, involving a compassionate self-forgiveness process, can diminish the struggle and suffering within your spirit, and then offer you greater insight and understanding of your purpose and value within the world. Writing about the depth of transformation occurring within the human psyche demands deep contemplation mindful attention and intention. Staying in the game means playing each move.

Although Mom was extremely competitive and went for the kill—truly, she had no mercy—she insisted on good sportsmanship. She saw you as an opponent and a friendly ally who would help her learn and grow through the challenges presented to her.

Playing games with my mom taught me how to show up even with adversity. I see the challenge, and maybe the discomfort, but I move forward anyway because it's through the engagement in the full experience that elevates life and deepens the connection within relationships. I learned to speak up and challenge things my mom said that were unexpected and felt 'off' with courage, strength, and conviction, yearning for the truth.

Courageously examining, gleaning, and acting on your grief insights and moving in the direction of your inner spirit's call converts your pain into gratitude, appreciation, and connection with your loved one who has died. You are *not* betraying your loved one by moving from mourning the loss to dancing with spirit. You are carrying the torch that has been passed on to you, living out their legacy, honoring them, and often fulfilling tasks at the next higher level. Our loved ones complete their life tasks to the degree they are able, and then, through the revelations of our grief journey, we connect to their legacy and our role in continuing family traditions.

My writing hiatus—in my mind, avoidance—actually became an internal experience of mining for precious gems. The twists and turns of my internal emotional rollercoaster were the transformations preparing me to reveal and share my moxie.

For a month or so, I was dealing with stomach issues that came on acutely at the end of 2020. In conjunction with a series of medical diagnostic tests, I engaged in numerous processes to explore my inner spiritual landscape to discover how my current experiences might be connected to the physical upheaval.

As Gabor Maté, retired Canadian physician and trauma expert, said directly to me in a virtual workshop on trauma, "What are you having trouble digesting?" and "What can't you stomach?" These are powerful out-of-the-box questions that can help us connect more deeply within our bodies.

Interestingly, I am writing about my mom—my grief, our relationship, our life patterns together—and she had major stomach issues. Mom had bellyaches galore that always popped up Friday nights about the time Shabbat came in and my stepfather, Jeff, prepared to leave for the synagogue. I thought Mom just didn't like going to services, but now I wonder if some inner voice was calling for her attention at that time.

Given that my mom has been my muse, the similarities were striking. In the discomfort within my transformational process—my budding creativity—I was ever-so-gently nudged to seek God even more. I have been called to courageously stand up, speak out, take risks, and trust that God has truly blessed me with incredible talents, skills, and a divinely inspired message to share with the world. In conversation, this has been one of God's messages:

Good morning, Candi,
You have to listen inwardly. Come to Me. I am Your Source, Your Breath, Your Life Force. Do Not Look Outside Yourself. Do Not Compare. You are Enough. You are Precious.
Love, God

The ongoing multifaceted upheaval throughout our country called on me to draw deeply on my own moral and ethical integrity and responsibility, causing me to examine the meaning of my inner turmoil. Exploring our inner disturbance, gut or otherwise, leads us to align and connect with our internal moral compass. Mom always told me, "Listen to your gut." I was having difficulty digesting the world's challenges, but I found that listening to and exploring beneath the physical and emotional disturbance allowed me to discover my own soul's calling.

It's difficult for me to give a specific story of when Mom used this instruction. It truly became background noise and resurfaced in my grief as a directive for me to attune to the sensations within my body as a mechanism for inner guidance. This book is not a story about my mom, per se, or anyone in particular, but rather how our life becomes an illustration of what we've absorbed—the beliefs, patterns, and practices we've learned to live by from those we've encountered. This grief process has given me an opportunity to connect with my mom's soul essence and the pieces of wisdom she intended to offer me. . . even when I resisted it.

Someone will always be ahead of or behind us. How can we accept our path? One of my life lessons has been to be okay with where I am at any given time along life's journey. My ultimate magical wish would be to rejoice in each day, appreciate all my learning to date, release my longing to strive more, and graciously accept my lot in life.

Is it possible that the vicissitudes of life—the ebb and flow—are purposeful? Can we rejoice every day, appreciate all our lessons, never strive to achieve more, and be fully content?

It's not the endeavor we want to release, but rather, the struggle. These so-called words of encouragement did not feel purposeful or valuable initially. Moreover, they were stored within my psyche for a later time. At different times these words may have been offered by my parents, I don't think I knew their meaning and needed more guidance. It is only now that I can recognize and appreciate the value of my parents' intentional or unintentional teachings. This is the beauty that comes from embracing our grief journey.

Inner yearnings are designed to infuse us with the oomph needed to accomplish new tasks, express ourselves, and make beautiful contributions to our world. That tremendous drive is the energy that propels us into great things. That internal fiery spirit is our moxie.

I can hear my mom's energy and enthusiasm saying, "Just do it."

I am also aware of my dad's encouraging words saying, "Do something every day toward your goals and play the cards you're dealt."

The energy of those words felt hollow when I doubted myself and was unaware of the divine power in the Universe. Later, these phrases became hallowed words, cheering me on, reminding me, fueling me, and revealing to me this divine power that is eternally guiding me.

American actress, comedian, and writer Amy Poehler wrote, "Great people do things before they are ready. They do things before they know they can do it. Doing what you're afraid of, getting out of your comfort zone, taking risks—that's what life is."

I certainly embarked on endeavors before I was ready—or had thought them through—because of the spark in my heart. I felt afraid. I then moved forward despite my fear, inching my way out of my comfort zone. If I waited until all my ducks were in a row, I would never do anything.

Going forward with fear takes courage to trust that if I fall, there is a divine safety net to catch me. When I fall, I need to learn something from the experience. I gain strength by asking to be shown the lesson, picking myself up after the fall, recognizing that I am not too bruised to try again, and realigning to take my next steps.

Years after my father's death, I learned that he was amazed by my ability to take risks. I would jump and always land on my feet—like quitting a job without having a new one.

I have trusted my inner spirit to tell me when it was time to make a change. The only time I ever hesitated to leave a job, knowing I needed to move on, I was fired. My mom—without much empathy for my bruised ego—noted, "You wanted to leave anyway." Mom had lost a portion of her social filter by this time.

Even with that traumatic experience and a bruised ego, I realized the value in the experience from two of my favorite sayings, "God does for us what we cannot do for ourselves," and "Life's rejections are God's protections." These quotes reminded me to recognize the divine perfection and sacred gifts in being terminated from that job. God was protecting me from an unaligned environment by making it possible for me to leave.

I also realized that in trying to line up a new position first, I was attempting to act responsibly and do the right thing according to my family's belief pattern. Experiences like this teach me to live in alignment with my values and to trust my life course and inner knowing.

To expand our spiritual consciousness and receive the richness of the grief journey, we must listen for the call to our soul, answer the tone, attune to the message, and accept the divine appointment with undaunting courage. Embodying the boldness of moxie and trusting that even through our pain and discomfort, purpose and value await us.

Chapter 4

GRIEF IS A UNIQUE SPIRITUAL JOURNEY

"Just as a dying person will transition from a physical existence into their pure soul essence, we too, in our grief, transition from experiencing our loved one in a physical way to knowing their spiritual presence."

—Chaplain Candi Wuhrman

I would ask my mom, "What do you think happens when we die?" She would respond in a very matter-of-fact way, "We just die. That's it."

I would gingerly and with some hesitation say, "Well, what if there was more, and we didn't just die? Have you ever thought about that?"

Early on, she would shut me down in half a second. "Candi, that's it."

I would give one more nudge at that moment (I learned from the best!) and say, "Well, you'll have to let me know when you get there... wherever there is!"

Mom was uncomfortable talking about death and dying, which is not an unusual perspective for many people. Some cultures are more accepting and consciously aware. In hospice, we have a particular language that specifies distinct phases of death and dying, such as *transitioning* and *actively dying.* Oddly, many people want to talk *around* death and dying and avoid these words for fear that their mere mention will bring about the event or process more quickly.

For years, Mom would express to my sister Cathy, with great agitation, her dislike of the word *transition.* Mom never really identified her specific discomfort with the word, but I suspect that she either was afraid or it was a little too mystical for her. And so, I had to find other words that would describe the changes occurring in her last phase of life that would invite further conversation. I would try phrases like 'as your body declines, as you change, as your life comes to completion here on earth' just to name a few.

My sisters and I knew Mom was declining physically and mentally, although she could still beat me at cards—Gin, Rummy, Spit, and, of course, Poker. The mental faculties accessed in playing cards must be either automatic or psychic because she rarely missed a beat when it came to cards—any game, any time. Going for that next win and the engagement always brought her joy.

Even when she easily became confused and lost, Mom still tried to cajole her way to the casinos. She still had a fiery winning spirit and swore that her children's birth dates would be *the* winning numbers on her lottery tickets. Mom wanted to go to the casino just weeks before she died and attempted to convince us she was fine to be dropped off. Mom would deny that she ever moseyed over to the next poker table or slot machine, leaving her purse behind.

I have often shared with my patients and their families that death is a process, not an event. A person's decline can occur over a long period, and the actual dying process can take weeks. When we begin to see changes, this is the time for loved ones to gather around for heartfelt sharing and honoring relationships.

Anticipatory grief is the series of thoughts that surface as we contemplate the loss of our loved ones before the actual absence occurs and the expected emotions arise with the idea of living without them. One might even call anticipatory grief preemptive or preliminary grief. We may also begin to anticipate the loss of opportunities for a better relationship, and experience a loss of hope because the time for healing the relationship may be running out.

One morning, about a week after Mom was admitted to hospice, I was standing in my kitchen in Portland, preparing to make the trip to Tulsa for Mom's 91st birthday weekend. I burst into tears and heard my voice saying, "Mama, Mama, Mama," over and over again. I felt about three years old at that moment.

Awareness of anticipatory grief can be a time of preparing for someone's completion of life, both for the dying person and the family. Allowing the emotions to surface and beginning to acknowledge how deeply a person has touched our spirit connects us more fully to our hearts, the depth of love within our souls, and the impact the relationship has had in our lives.

So often, we're afraid of love. We want love, yet the magnitude and impact of the experiences are indescribably powerful. Love's journey in all its facets creates feelings of vulnerability and lack of control. At times, there are no words which can feel scary and unsettling. These anticipatory experiences of surfacing grief are sacred times with our loved ones to express the difficulty we feel in articulating our vulnerability and uncertainty.

While at the bedside of a family, two sons were in tears as their father neared death. Seemingly comfortable, their father was surprisingly still with us, but his children were suffering with grief. I shared with them that one's timing at the end of life is particularly sacred and divine—certainly not orchestrated by science or medicine, but something greater.

There was a sense of his sons holding something that weighed heavily upon them. As we spoke more of the family's journey through their struggles, experiences were revealed that needed to be forgiven and released, which then allowed them to let go and their father to die peacefully and with greater ease.

Often, people come to me as their parents are aging and they contemplate their expected emotions and wonder what life would be like without their loved ones. These experiences of anticipatory grief bring questions of being loved. Will they miss their parents and in what ways? Will they be devastated, functional, or in a puddle of tears? We tend to freeze, constrict, and hold our breath as we question our anticipated experiences.

Anticipatory Grief is…

- awakening to the reality that our parents, spouses, and any dear ones will not live in their bodies forever.
- when a loved one receives a diagnosis, our fear level rises with the awakening of an eventual loss.
- the recognition that life could be much shorter than what we once thought.
- an awakening to our lack of control and a sense of powerlessness.
- a realization that our parents, spouses, siblings, and friends may have chosen life patterns and practices that may shorten their lives.

Anticipatory grief is purposeful. It forces us to pay attention to our emotions and begin to grieve. In that emotion, we begin to recognize how much we care and are invested in the relationship—how much we love, still want to be loved, and still want to love. Anticipatory grief begins to help us recognize our mortality, fallibility, and vulnerability.

It helps us recognize that we will grieve when our loved one dies, and it helps us somewhat prepare by creating a support network, merely by acknowledging loss as a part of life. We love so therefore we will grieve and will need something, even if we don't yet know what that will be.

We've made a valuable investment of love and time and then realize our physical time together will someday come to an end. So we begin to feel a sense of urgency and try to squeeze in more experience, fearing that we've inadequately shared life. We question whether we've done enough—often, we have. However, we can be terrified about the unknown reality of a pending loss, the absence of our loved one, and knowing that there will always be more that we'll want to share.

Anticipatory grief can catch us off guard at the oddest times and in the weirdest ways as we recognize how deeply connected we are to another human. I experienced fear which produced a surprising episode of early grief related to my husband, Arnie, when he had to be taken to the emergency room. Fortunately, his condition was not life-threatening, but the experience reminded me once again of life's fragile, uncertain, and unpredictable nature. We cannot predict how long we will live. Once I examined this experience, I could see my anticipated grief surfacing.

Moments when I recognize my grief and acknowledge its .presence, although vulnerable and sometimes scary, are truly precious. I know that it occurs because I have opened my heart to fully love. Becoming more aware of how deeply connected I am with my husband has been both comforting and unsettling. Often in that uncertainty, I may become agitated or angry. I am fully aware that beneath my anger is often fear, and my fear of loss has surfaced. To put it plainly, I know I will experience pain when my husband dies if he dies before me. Although my preference would be for us to die together, that would be more painful for our children.

The truth is that we cannot plan for these things. As we age, we become more aware of the physical changes we are experiencing. If I hear a noise from Arnie's office or outside after he has just left, I check to make sure he is okay. Even when I am in the shower and hear a crash, my immediate response now is to check on him. When I call out and don't hear a response, I have to decide whether to finish my shower before visually checking or calling out a bit louder. If I wait too long, and he is really in trouble, he could die. Anything can happen, and I have to walk myself through the inevitable.

When Arnie dies, I will be okay. Of course, it's good to know that I am not ready for my husband to leave this earth. At the same time, I believe these thoughts and processes surface to help us prepare. I intend to remember that I am not in control of these big unpredictable things—often the little ones either. I plan to live each day to the fullest.

Recognizing the thoughts and emotions surfacing as our loved one's time in the physical body is ending is anticipatory grief. At every phase, I encourage family members to allow deep emotions to surface as they are necessary and valuable in easing the shock. Taking deep breaths while facing a loved one's dying experience opens the heart to be more present with the one we love and will miss.

Anticipatory grief is an opportunity to arrange support for the grief journey by acknowledging the impending loss and taking dominion over it. We can't prepare for the loss in one sense, because we know we *will* feel the absence. However, we can prepare for our accompaniment to assist us in honoring our grief process.

Asking for help is difficult for most of us. I knew I would need help when my mom died but wouldn't know what or how until the time came.

My dear friend Ronda and I discussed my anticipated need a few years before Mom died. Ronda committed without hesitation to do whatever I might need as I returned to my life in Portland.

Sitting at Mom's kitchen table after she died, surrounded by boxes, I pondered returning to Portland alone with complete horror. Only then did I begin to realize what I needed. Ronda flew from Denver to Portland, met me in baggage claim, helped me with several bags, rode the train with me, walked from the train station to my office where my car was parked, got me home, and helped me restock my fridge with food.

I was so grateful I had asked for help. Her presence carried me into the first stage of mourning.

The grief journey is a spiritual transformation—an exploration of our inner landscape. As I mentioned earlier, death is a process, not an event, and the same is true for spiritual transformation.

Transformation is a process, and change does not happen overnight. If it did, physical exercise would be a breeze. Personal growth and inner change—spiritual transformation—is a lifetime of small, cumulative shifts within our psyche.

Talking about death with Mom was so important. Quite honestly, many people don't realize that a dying person grieves leaving their life and those they love. Mom thought about dying but didn't know how to articulate her concerns, which were the unknown aspects of the dying process and her reluctance to leave her children. I believe she didn't want to scare us by talking about death.

I would remind Mom that she would be able to talk to me in some way after she died. I would ask her if she had any wishes. I never missed an opportunity to call whenever I thought of her.

My dad died much earlier than my mom. After Dad's ALS (Amyotrophic Lateral Sclerosis) diagnosis, I decided to call him whenever he came to mind. Calling him worked well and gave us opportunities for sacred conversations. With my mom, I would share my thoughts and my grief by telling her often how much I loved her and that I would miss her terribly when she was gone.

From my hospice experience, I find most people think about death and dying. They wonder what their dying process will be, if they have done enough, and if their family will be okay.

As our anticipation of a loss arises, we need to speak to our loved ones. We won't scare them by talking about death and dying. It is liberating to have these discussions. Death and dying conversations are sacred and courageous. Connecting through these heartfelt talks gives our loved ones a gift.

Although often these are tearful conversations, freedom and relief do come, which in turn make the person's dying process and the family's grief much easier.

For years, I wanted to arrive at a place of perfection within my relationships and not have to work so hard. But there is no perfect place—that's the ego striving for utopia. There is no real imperfection either; it is all perfectly divine.

Life is a perfectly imperfect process. That doesn't mean everything is always easy and joyful. We experience hardship and difficulty and seek the lessons that our souls can learn from these challenges.

I want to be very clear and transparent: loss is excruciating—it is real pain and sorrow. We often feel victimized by the absence of a person: mother, father, sister, brother, child, young or old. Through the grief process, often fraught with simultaneously opposing experiences, we come to accept the loss as a necessary transition. Trust the timing. The seemingly unfair measure of pain and all-too-soon absence of a loved one becomes the means for bringing greater good to both us and the world. Embracing the grief journey opens us up to what the death of our loved ones is teaching us about living our lives.

Grief is an appropriate emotional response to loss. There are many losses to grieve, including a loved one, our childhood, a career, a relationship, a hope, and a dream. Grief begins when we contemplate an upcoming loss or feel a pang of emptiness deep within our gut, a sense that something is slipping away.

We know we are all going to die at some point, but we don't know when or how. God, Our Creator, Divine Source, or Higher Power will determine when we've completed our earthly tasks and reveal to us that it's time to go on to our next journey.

What we do know is that the thought of being without someone we love is painful.

Very soon after my dad died, I enrolled in a week-long grief workshop in Tucson, Arizona. Immersing myself in the grief intensive was the greatest gift I could have given myself at that time. I remember a very specific exercise where I wrote two letters to my dad, one from my younger self and another from my adult self, which I prepared to read to him imagining him in an empty chair. Twenty-six years later, most of the details escape me, except that my younger self shared how I felt abandoned and hurt and wanted more from my dad. However, the letter as my adult self, the woman that I had become, was able to release my dad to the universe and tell him I would be bringing his grandchild into the world—although I was not yet pregnant at that time.

After reading these letters aloud symbolically to my dad in the grief group, I saw my dad walking away—strong, vibrant, and free. This was particularly shocking since the progression of his moderately advanced ALS had caused significant muscle weakness and nerve breakdown until his ultimate death from a heart attack. Dad couldn't walk alone and had become dependent on a walker. My dad's soul walked away free from the physical confinement of his disease.

Years later, during the early stages of grief after my mother's death, I discovered Judy Unger, an artist who wrote meditation songs after her son's death. These songs helped her connect with Spirit, transported her through her grief, and allowed her to feel her son's essence. One particular song called "Set You Free" spoke to the power of seeing and feeling our loved one's spiritual essence when we physically set them free.

Unger wrote, "I would never forget his essence, smile, voice, and face. He was irreplaceable. It turned out that setting him free ultimately set me free."

These words resonated with me and my grief experience with my dad. Processing the inner pain through the layers of grief and loss allowed me to walk freely and see the good in the relationship and the soulful beauty of my loved one.

Releasing hurt, anger, and resentment opens the flow of love and joy. During that week-long grief intensive workshop, I shared a great deal of childhood pain and what I had hoped the relationship with my father could have been. This freed both my dad and me and opened my soul to more love.

Over time, with a lot of processing and deep healing, I was able to better know my dad's essence, smile, laugh, face, voice, and strength, even after he was no longer physically present.

I am aware of my capricious nature in recalling
my grief journey without any chronological value.
Organically, my brain is attempting to organize
an unstructured, disorganized series of experiences
within the grief process. The grief journey and spiritual
transformation are not linear, succinct, or ordered
and often appear and feel messy. Grief from death
can trigger losses from earlier ages in our lives,
a depth of loneliness from the loss of connection
throughout our lives, and even the loss of oneself.

Understand that I'm a feeler through and through, and so was my mom. She got teased when she was emotional, as did I. I feel most things very deeply.

One friend used to tell me, "The good news is you feel everything, and the bad news is you feel everything."

I judged myself for many years for my sensitivity and how deeply I was touched. Today, I know that being a feeler is my superpower. Feeling deeply helps me connect with all aspects of myself, alerts me to the fact that my attention is needed, helps me relate to others quickly, and aligns me with my inner divine power easily. We never need to apologize for our emotions. In a relationship, feeling an emotional experience viscerally indicates a depth of impact and connection.

Grief is unpredictable, chaotic, and confusing. I like to look good and appear together (even when I'm not), but the truth is that I can make up my face, dress in my best—pressed and shiny—and internally be twisted in knots and feel upside down.

So, if you feel like your insides are jumbled and falling apart, consider the possibility that what is unraveling is a part of you that needs healing and may just be falling away. Remember, after a loss, our internal systems have to recalibrate without the regular engagement of our loved one's physical presence. From my own experience, I found that I needed to unravel to transform my inner being. Accepting the inner turmoil as purposeful and embracing the changes that occurred within my whole being (whether I liked them or not) became my north star, my guiding light, in my grief healing.

My pain directed my path toward deepening my faith, strengthening my resilience, and empowering me more than I ever could have imagined.

There is purpose and value in pain. At times, I experienced deep sorrow and longing for my mom's soft touch and enveloping hugs. In the past, her embrace felt suffocating, but now, I yearned for that warmth and comfort.

I would write letters to her during my morning meditation, crying and trying to understand what was happening to me. I knew there was a purpose in this grief process and was committed to going through all that I needed to emerge with a deeper understanding. The pain of her absence felt excruciating.

Feeling into and connecting with the emotions that surface is the path of least resistance. We humans often want to be composed, controlled thinkers, and don't like showing our vulnerability appearing messy. However, this is how the heart heals. The unpredictable unfolding of grief waves can be unsettling, but if we ride the waves to their peak through the dark, cold tunnels, we often receive profound awareness and remarkably clear messages when we enter into the sunlight again.

Showing emotions is vulnerable, and often the expression of emotions is thought of as a sign of weakness. Releasing deep emotions can clear the path for a renewed sense of strength, empowerment, and joy to assist us in taking our next steps.

One day during one of my yoga classes, I was introduced to a beautiful song by Christina Perri called "A Thousand Years." I began to sob uncontrollably—quietly, although constantly sniffling—throughout the class. Tears and sweat covered my yoga mat. It was such a huge release.

Some folks might avoid intense crying at all costs. In my mind, a song that allows me to release deep emotions is a gift and serves as a vehicle to help me navigate my grief and holds value for profound grief messages.

I started playing the song regularly as I wrote Mom letters in my morning quiet time. As I listened one morning, crying, I wrote, *Mama, where are you? I know you're there. I can't see you. I want to hug you, feel you, hear you. Where are you?*

I can only describe my gut disturbance as a huge excavation project. Mom always said, "Listen to your gut!" *The feelings in my gut are turning me upside down. What is happening?*

Generally speaking, most of us hold our breath waiting for the pain of loss to pass. The foreboding grief emotions accumulate in the pit of our stomachs, as a lump in our throats, a heaviness in our chests, and tears that well up in our eyes. Grief touches every part of our lives because the memories of those we love are imprinted on our souls. I often share with those grieving that we grieve so deeply because we've loved so greatly, and yet, we wouldn't trade the love for the loss. If we knew there was purpose in the grief journey, and that on the other side of the pain would be some beautiful, amazing awareness, we would be more open to the discomfort associated with the healing process.

Even when we think we are done with a relationship and truly want to be free of the pain, there may be yet another layer of grief. We cannot face all of our life experiences in one fell swoop, as life's events are often revealed one piece at a time. As new losses occur and we continue to do our inner work, we will have a new understanding of life's events, which allows us to then be more receptive to our loved one's spiritual essence.

Each person's experiences with loss vary. During the darkest period of this grief journey, I felt very insecure, meek, and uncertain—a state I would rather not revisit. The imbalance of this endless pain was scary and destabilizing, whereas my normal disposition had been a state of equanimity—calm and emotionally balanced. As the Christina Perri song so aptly called into question, I did not know how to be brave, and that quality was not even in my present consciousness. The bigger question was how could I love again?

This song was about romantic love, and I had lost my mom, so how exactly did this apply? My heart was broken; that was real and understandable, but I didn't understand why this song struck such a chord in me.

After Mom died, I was afraid, but this song's premise didn't make sense in its intended context. I kept listening because I knew it was speaking to my spirit; there was something about love, and playing it repeatedly, that made me feel closer to Mom.

I was grieving deeply because I'd loved so greatly.

Love? If this pain was the result of love, then, thanks, but I'll pass. Similar to the song lyrics, I felt as though I was standing alone with a whole lot of doubt in the world and dreading the days ahead, and no one could know the pain I was feeling. This song spoke the truth of my inner experience; my inner turmoil, my fragility, and my unsteadiness to take steps forward to discover what this grief was teaching me. I didn't feel a promise of a brighter tomorrow.

In the initial phases of grief (the first year and some of the second year), feeling Mom's physical absence each day was excruciatingly painful.

I didn't know why I kept repeatedly listening and crying to this song, over and over again—sometimes with lyrics and at other times, the instrumental version. Some might wonder why I was seemingly torturing myself by engaging in this practice (and it truly became a practice) over and over.

It didn't feel like torture, and I knew I was supposed to trust the process, so I kept on. Listening and connecting repeatedly felt like tuning into a recording that had a subliminal message. The experience drew me in. Somehow, the crying washed away any blocks that might have prevented me from hearing divine communication. *Was it Mom? Was it God?*

Each deep emotional wave of grief that I survived moved me closer and closer to knowing my mom's love more than I did previously. This nonlinear, capricious unfolding process awakened me to the gifts God and my mom had bestowed upon me. The love spoken in the lyrics of "A Thousand Years" is the endless, everlasting, unconditional loving presence that is universal and within each human being's divine essence—not just in some, but in all.

Christina Perri's song lyrics speak of a belief that there is no time, everything stands still, all is beautiful, and that in every breath and every hour, the life of a spirit—a soul—is everlasting.

We all possess timeless beauty and sharing it with the world demands bravery. My mom's beauty was endless. I mainly saw her physical beauty. She was always dressed to the nines wearing vibrant colors with gorgeous glowing skin, and bright red lipstick. She had a smile and laugh that lit up a room and would listen to your story as if you were the only person in the world. But I had not yet learned to see her as a beautiful soul. She had been my mom just nudging me through life.

My insecurities and spiritual immaturity once questioned Mom's love. Now I see that her nudging was her attention and love guiding me through life.

Although I no longer cry when I play this song, the words still touch me deeply and infuse every cell of my being with powerful, vibrant, loving energy. This song stirred the waves of grief within my spirit that ignited my healing journey.

While my mom was dying, she went through an unraveling process, and I, too, was unraveling for several months after she died. Everything that was, wasn't anymore. Everything was different. I knew I would grieve, but I didn't know what this round of grief would be like. Twenty-three years had passed since Dad had died. I worked with death, dying, grief, and loss daily, and I knew that grief was inevitable and unavoidable. However, I didn't yet know what type of emotional support I needed for the journey.

I had just moved to Oregon only six months before Mom died, made some friends, and was supported by my hospice colleagues, but I hadn't yet felt a need to seek a therapist or counselor. Even though I had a lot of grief education, training, and processing skills, it was becoming clear that I needed help, and someone to be a witness to my grief process. I needed someone to hear me, see me, and listen to my stories. It's important to tell your story. I didn't need someone to tell me what I should do, or how I should feel, and I most definitely didn't need fixing. I wasn't broken as a person. My heart was broken. I was sad and hurt. There's a significant difference. The right help is appropriate and everyone's needs are different.

One morning, just after a shower, I stood completely naked in front of my open closet, tears running down my face, needing to get dressed but completely unable to choose my clothing for the day. Unexpectedly, my good friend Liora called, and I answered the call crying, sharing my nakedness, my indecisiveness, and the feeling that I was unraveling. I felt scared and uncomfortable. As I began to acknowledge the validity of my grief process, it was understandable that I would be having this experience of unraveling. A sort of unwinding of all the years of life experiences with my mom seemed very understandable, but surprisingly unexpected.

My unraveling during these early times of grief seemed to be a life review of my experiences with my mom, revealing the many ways she had affected my life. The overwhelming and powerful revelation after my mom's death was recognizing and feeling my mom's imprint on every part of my soul—whether I had wanted it or not.

Geographically, we lived thousands of miles apart for most of my adult life. However, my mom had been with me for fifty-six years—my whole life—and we were energetically connected. Of course, I was unraveling.

Although I was seemingly falling apart and in the depths of my pain, I was completely aware that Mom had died on the right day, January 18, 2018. The number eighteen is important in Judaism. The Hebrew word *chai* translates to "life" with the two Hebrew letters equaling the numerical value of eighteen. I found profound meaning and reassurance in the divine connection to the time of her death, and yet, I still had to go through my feelings of loss. Recognizing these significant signs can bring value, comfort, and support while still addressing discomfort.

Here's a journal entry in the depths of my longing trying to understand my loss:

February 22, 2018

Mom, I didn't know I would miss your physical presence so much, but I do. I thought because I understood death and the dying process and had experienced the spiritual realm and presence of people so readily, I wouldn't feel so sad and miss you so much...but I do. I miss your whole presence: being able to hear your voice, have a conversation, feel your touch, the warmth of your hands and hugs holding me. I miss you gently moving my hair out of my face, your smile, and your "Hi, Baby!" each time I called you. I love you so much, Mom. I never thought I'd love you so much.

I let you in. I know you permeated my entire being. You saw right through my façade. I let my armor down and allowed myself to be vulnerable. I'm sad I couldn't do it sooner and have more time to know you and love you. I'm so grateful to have had all the wonderful times we've had and to learn how to love and be loved. I know a depth of love that is incredible.

I hope I will love my kids as much as you've loved me,
and that they'll allow me to be in their lives and
to love them in the healthiest and most joyful ways.

Thank you, Mama. You are incredible.
Let's keep talking. I love you.

Engaging in spiritual transformation while processing a loss requires us to unwind and untangle the experience of knowing a person solely in physical form and then opening up to their spiritual essence.

As a human spirit begins to disconnect from the physical existence in the dying process—which can be disconcerting—the soul is awakening and preparing for a whole new world of adventure and will begin to take flight in an entirely different way. We too, in our grief, do the same. Our soul transforms and reconfigures for a new adventure in life. The experiences that occur resonate because of their familiarity with our real-life memories of our loved ones. The fuel of the spirit presence of our loved one guides our transformational journey to awaken to a spiritual presence beyond our comprehension and is distinctly undeniable.

Waves of grief often come out of nowhere and knock us off our feet emotionally. The sensation can be a whole-body experience, often taking us to an earlier time in our lives. It is not unusual for me to access an earlier age: an experience, memory, or emotional state. The experiences used to scare me as I thought I was regressing.

Early in my self-discovery, I'd interpreted from psychological professionals that regressing to an earlier time in my life was a sign of a poor mental status. Based on years of experience revisiting my younger years and healing my wounds at a soul level, I guard against labels because I know how valuable and productive the experiences can be. I now engage in the experiences for their deep therapeutic healing benefits.

However, if while processing your younger memories, you have a fear or concern for your safety, I would always recommend that you seek professional assistance from a chaplain, counselor, or therapist to navigate the journey more easily. To be aware and be able to address your age-related experiences is a healthy processing tool. We never have to be alone in our healing. Please acknowledge your experiences as valuable and ask for support to honor yourself and your journey.

Looking back on one of my previously mentioned moments of anticipatory grief as my mom entered hospice care, I remembered the power of bursting into tears as I felt about three years old calling out to my mom.

I'd been comforting and honoring my patients' family's grief for years, saying, "Of course, you're hurting deeply, it's your mom. She's imprinted your entire being throughout your whole life, even when you haven't been physically near her."

Now, I was viscerally feeling my mom's imprint on me as early as three years old. I was keenly aware of how my mom had been with me my entire life. Even though there had been both good and bad times—times when she was more emotionally available than others—she was always in my life. She was my security and comfort when I was young and I was crying out for that again. The anticipatory grief felt excruciating and enlightening, as if I was connected to her beyond comprehension, science, and any linear logical sense.

In the depths of my despairing grief and wanting desperately to feel Mom's presence, I again began writing to her in my sacred quiet time when I sought divine connection and centering.

I would tell her whatever was in my heart: recent activities, emotions, and troubles. This was an organic process for me not difficult or odd — becuase for years I'd written letters to God in my meditation time and allowed God to write back. I describe this experience as a communication with God.

One name doesn't always fit for every experience or encounter. Divine Presence has many emanations—love, light, compassion, grace, spirit, holy, and sacred, to name a few. The emanations can be qualities, characteristics, or parts of universal creation, such as aspects of nature and celestial bodies. Each precious soul has the divine right to describe and define that sacred and holy presence with one name, many names, or a feeling that aligns with one's inner truth.

In my yearning and seeking to feel my mom's presence, I poured out my soul, engaging my whole being, and then, answers came.

Mom would write back to me. It was my handwriting but her words, such as "I'm here, Candy" (I changed the "Y" to an "I" in my twenties), "I'm here, Candela" (another endearing name), and "I'm here, Baby" (yet another one, because I was the baby of the family, although she would call my sisters Baby too). I would be contemplating doing something like writing this book or creating something, and I would hear, "Do it, just do it; what are you waiting for?" and know it was her. I could sense her energy.

Throughout my life, Mom was my biggest fan (although I didn't always believe that), especially with creative projects and actions that made me more visible in the world. Several years ago, when I was making Candiwraps (beautiful reversible sewn fabric shawls), Mom felt so strongly that I should take them further and offer them to large chain stores, but I never did. Then, at a later time, when I was considering my first series of grief groups, Mom very quickly and boldly encouraged me with a big "Yes, you should do it!"

While initially her nudges were annoying and felt controlling, I began to hear her differently—more nourishing, poignant, and powerful—with a shift in her energy. Her emphatic direct message felt loving, connected, and grounded—truly, divinely engaging. Something was changing.

Unfulfilled dreams are unexpressed divine energy—sometimes trapped in parts of the body, mind, and spirit—that spills out incrementally through life's encounters. That unexpressed energy is often projected onto another—often, our children—with expectations and hopes. This transference can sound like encouragement or feel like a push for us to accept a job, take an action, or make a move that is fueled by another's wistful longing for an unfulfilled dream.

Mom held a wondrous vision for my life. Many moms have wishes and dreams for their children, so this makes sense. However, I suspect her vision was more about her because I'd only just begun to explore life as an adult. While Mom thought I owned the world and could do anything, living my potential felt incomprehensible at those points in life.

Potential is unique for each person and something cannot be measured or rushed. As a little girl, I fearless and wanted to be a firefighter. As a teenager, I thought I knew everything and went into adulthood with a fiery attitude. Somewhere along the way, I discovered that I had insecurities and issues to work on—as we all do. Only as we grow and life unfolds organically, do we begin to see what the world has to offer and what we can offer the world.

Uncertainty, doubt, and struggle (otherwise known as growing pains) are exactly the grit that mold us into who we are meant to be. Raw gemstones become smooth and polished by using a rock tumbler with a grit mixture made of sand and gravel or by hand with sandpaper. I have tumbled with a lot of grit to face uncertainty and insecurities along my healing journey to grow, evolve, and become the healthiest person I could be.

My mom wanted me to embrace opportunities at times because she had not achieved fulfillment in certain areas. Over time, the energy of her encouragement shifted, and I came to experience her enthusiasm as a sense that she was metaphorically passing the torch of a vibrant light to me. My mom's hidden motivation fueled her encouragement, excitement, and enthusiasm. She may have been unknowingly, yet divinely, channeling her unexpressed moxie energy to me.

This new perspective is immensely valuable. I shifted my earlier belief from Mom trying to control aspects of my life experiences and pushing me towards activities or adventures she deemed exciting, to sharing the joy, power of enthusiasm, and infinite possibilities of life's creative expression.

What is now a beautiful and welcomed viewpoint, and an explanation for a repetitive, painful, and frustrating challenge with my mom, took years of therapy and deep spiritual healing work to achieve this shift in consciousness. Today, as an adult but still my parents' child, I can recognize the significant nudges as divine inspiration to propel me beyond where my parents left off, never losing momentum as they energetically pass the baton to us in life's marathon.

Stepping into my moxie has been a bigger task than I ever could have imagined. Although similar to many other times of transformation, in this unfolding process, the stirring and nudging felt much deeper. This segment of my grief transformation was expanding deep within my belly and was necessary for creating my fullest, vibrant life.

How is this relevant to the grief journey?

Pain is inevitable with a loss and the multiple losses that we will all endure throughout our lifetimes. The way we choose to face our loss will make all the difference.

During my writing journey, I attended a seminar in which the facilitator told a brief story about the way buffalo weather storms. I researched a bit further and discovered that cattle and buffalo can sense a storm brewing. Cattle run away from the storm, trying to outrun its force. Buffalo will turn and charge directly into the storm. Rory Vaden, in an article on overcoming adversity, shared that by running into the storm's course, the buffalo runs straight through it, minimizing the amount of pain, time, and frustration they experience from the storm.

This powerful metaphor and instinctive directive for human beings emphasizes that we will all have pain, and its duration can be lessened by going through it. From my own experience, I know that we can only heal our pain if we are willing to feel it.

Through our grief experience and transformation, we will inevitably receive sacred messages prompting internal change for our greater good. Recognizing and embracing our internal shifts, changes in our consciousness, and their effect on the world can become our guide to make our loved one's memory and legacy a blessing for the planet. This is rarely a straight course. Subtle messages from our loved ones and awareness from our waves of emotions are revealed in bits and pieces. Clarity and revelations come over time.

If we truly allow and embrace the spiritual transformation, we are becoming a newer, enhanced version of ourselves. We cannot stay the same. Even if you feel stuck in a particular stage of your journey, you're still moving forward. Your grief journey may feel like you're inching your way through thick mud or sinking in quicksand.

I have never experienced quicksand. However,
for many years of my childhood, I had a terrifying
recurring nightmare of sinking in it, so I am intimately
familiar with that horrifying threat.

You are not lost, nor are you drowning, dissolving, or wasting away. However, as you transform through grief, there is a lot to unpack and process, releasing the parts and patterns that you no longer need. The grief process is initially about the one who died—the excruciating pain you feel from the loss—and later it becomes more about who you have an opportunity to become.

Chapter 5

LEARNING BEFORE AND AFTER DEATH

"Death does not need to be a catastrophic, destructive thing: indeed, it can be viewed as one of the most constructive, positive, and creative elements of culture and life."

—Elisabeth Kubler-Ross

No one teaches us how to grieve a loved one. Grief is not just about an end. Grief is an experience that offers an opportunity to walk through the pain with purpose, to discover yourself, and ultimately, to live a more meaningful and authentic life. After a loss and living with grief, it feels like our heart is broken—like a flattened balloon—as if our breath has been knocked right out of us.

During my intense grief after my mom died, I sought to muster some strength and understanding that would make sense of my life. I didn't realize that my mom was the glue of our family and when our anchor was cut, we were adrift. Prior to my mom's death, my sister,

Cathy, and I would talk regularly about the changes we were seeing with our mom's health and simultaneously, I was walking with her through her husband's illness and decline. After Mom died, I needed to be present for my own grief and the breadth of my own emotions rather than be available to someone else. My sisters and I couldn't be there for each other and had to find our own grounding within our respective grief journeys.

My entire internal landscape was shifting, and I couldn't keep up. I didn't know how or where I'd find inspiration to feel alive again. I felt dead inside. Walking through the depths of my despair is what led me to find my inner strength, determination, and fiery spirit again.

As a hospice chaplain, sitting at the bedside of many patients and families facing the end of life and working with thousands of people through the layers of uncertainty as they grapple with grief and loss, I knew I would grieve my own loss but couldn't know what my personal journey ahead would look like. There had to be a purpose and value for going through this much pain. There had to be some divine meaning. I wanted to embrace the spiritual lessons of the entire journey.

Spirituality is an inner alignment to life's meaning within the heart and soul. Caroline Myss, author of *Anatomy of the Spirit,* says in an interview with Oprah that our spirit is the part of us that seeks meaning and purpose and is drawn to hope.

In the world of chaplaincy, we help people with their inner fire, divine light, and resonant truth to discover meaning and value in their lives. Often, our internal sensations become our guide. These feelings are our soul's awakenings. This experience is our soul talking to our bodies. We are not separate, but for many of us, we think we are a body first, and the soul just comes along for the ride. In actuality, the soul directs the body. If the body and soul were in greater harmony with one another, we would be healthier people on all levels: physically, emotionally, mentally, and spiritually.

We have a physical existence on this planet, but our soul is what brings life. Our very breath of life is filled with purpose, value, and our drive for living—the force that reveals our moxie. This experience of the soul may be enhanced or guided by our involvement in religious practice but might not be governed by religious constructs.

Religion is a set of beliefs, traditions, and practices that may direct our thinking, provide an order or structure for a value-based life, and lead us toward a holy connection. Spirituality is engaging in a relationship with a sacred source of strength, connection, and power that guides and deepens our awareness of life, the value of life, and the meaning and purpose of our life on Earth. For some, this power has a name, and for others, it does not. All are acceptable because your life journey is the evolution of your inner spirit, which is, in essence, your spirituality.

When a death occurs, we have the opportunity to open up to a greater experience of the components within the spiritual realm. We shift from knowing our loved ones solely in a physical way—seeing, hearing, feeling, and touching them; connecting with our bodily physical senses—to knowing them outside of those sensory spaces only our bodies can provide for us.

When we move from physical to spiritual, we expand our senses and consciousness. Our awareness attunes as our loved ones nudge us and play with us energetically by sending us messages such as when I described the spiritual experience of playing the word moxie during a Scrabble game just two months after my mom died. This experience gave me the profound and palpable sense of my mom's spiritual presence with me.

Spiritual conversations may seem esoteric or too out of the box. We search for words to describe the intangible, unexplainable, ineffable, and unseen. Who dares to admit to the tickle on our arm in the middle of the day out of nowhere?

Much of spirituality can seem mysterious and inaccessible. However, the intangible and unseen can become real and accessible simply by acknowledging that there is another layer of energetic presence available that explains the unexplainable and has the potential to enrich us and bring meaning and purpose to our lives.

Our soul continues. Nurturing the spirit helps us prepare for the inevitable closure of life. Sacred conversations are a process of spirit discovery. Sometimes, until we begin talking to and asking questions with our loved ones and ourselves about our thoughts and beliefs about death and dying, we don't know the deep essence of another.

One of my favorite questions to ask my patients is, "What do you think happens when we die?"

One of the most precious answers from one ninety-six-year-old patient was, "I don't know, I've never done it." This woman was already spiritually transitioning, and I experienced her soul traveling between both worlds—the physical and the spiritual. This patient would tell me that she was seeing her deceased parents sitting at the next table and outside her childhood home with incredible descriptions—very palpable, precise, and present. Her childhood home was detailed to a T. When I clarified with her family, her visuals were remarkably accurate. What was interesting was she was completely immersed in this visualization as if it were in the present day. She desperately wanted to get to her parents but was unaware that they were just out of her reach in the spiritual realm. She couldn't see these experiences as beyond her physical world.

My patient was religious but not spiritual. She connected and aligned with a very specific set of beliefs. Anything outside of those tangible constructs was too vague and esoteric to fathom.

My inquiry is genuine. I am truly interested in one's innermost thoughts about death, awareness of the dying process, and beliefs about an afterlife. I will also sometimes lightly dance around the subject and gently invite someone to share their experiences of loss and the meaning of those deaths.

There are many different views on dying and concepts on life after death—an afterlife—such as if there is one, and if so, what it might look like. However, some people don't deeply contemplate the reality beyond accepting that one day we will no longer exist in this world. That is as far as it goes—a "here today, gone tomorrow" end-of-life concept. Others may wonder, if the soul continues to exist, then in what way?

A lot transpires within a person physically and spiritually in the last phase of life. *As a person declines, internally they are contemplating their departure—a trip beyond all adventures—and wonder about the destination ahead.* Communication is different. Sometimes, a person's actual language will return to their native tongue; their tone may sound childlike, fearful, or angry.

Transition is occurring on many levels. We might describe this as our psyche dying bit by bit where we are shedding parts of ourselves that are no longer needed for the journey into a purely spiritual existence.

Our Creator—our Source of Life—is the very breath that is blown into us every few seconds.

The length of days on Earth is uncertain for us all. We think a good life is a long life, and what defines "long" is different in each of our minds.

We have no idea how long we'll live, and we are all here for specific reasons that are not up to us. We're all spiritual beings having an earthly human existence.

My mom loved musicals and, more specifically, show tunes. She claimed she couldn't carry a tune. However, she carried a tune in her heart and a spring in her step.

My mom was okay with leaving this world and knew it was time, but she still had a zest for living. Better said, she didn't want to leave those she loved, and she still held an appreciation for life. Mom's zest for life was energized by dance scenes and music in her heart and soul. Every time Mom heard a musical tune she'd light up and would even dance in her seat when she was no longer steady on her feet. Those tunes always reminded her of her years of dancing and teaching dance. The vibrant energy of show tunes filled her spirit and brought her alive.

For many years, my mom and I had a challenging relationship, and I wondered how I'd feel when she died. Of course, I didn't know how long either one of my parents would live, and I'd hoped to be in a state of gratitude and appreciation for both of them at the end of their lives.

My dad was diagnosed with ALS soon after my husband, Arnie, and I married in June of 1993. Dad's diagnosis gave me time to consider that he might not live forever.

I remember telling Arnie one day after the diagnosis, "I'm going to call my dad whenever I think of him." And that's exactly what I did. Of course, not knowing what the future would hold, I wanted to take every opportunity to connect. That idea must have been divine inspiration because that wasn't where my heart was truly at the time.

I had a lot to walk through over the years with my dad—my parents' divorce, my dad's anger, and being scared of him for many years. Being the youngest, I had a very different experience than my older sisters, and there were many things I didn't know about him or his view of our family's life.

In 1994, I asked my dad questions like, "You know that movie *Mississippi Burning*? Well, I was born in 1961, and the movie portrays the South in 1963 when we lived in Mississippi. What was it like? Did you see that type of slavery and discrimination?"

He'd tell me stories of our life there at that time and how the board of his hospital wanted him to construct separate entrances—one black and one white—and he wouldn't do it. As a Jew who fled Germany in 1939 and a victim of discrimination, he wouldn't inflict the same on another human being. He found ways around such exclusion.

Through these multiple conversations, I felt my dad's presence more consistently. In former years, I'd only felt that sporadically. A new, welcomed connection was established.

After living with ALS for over a year, he died suddenly from a heart attack in November of 1994. I was only thirty-three years old when he died at the age of sixty-six, but I was very grateful to have taken the time to talk to him.

My grief for my dad at this time was filled with an awareness of loss and also freedom after having done a great deal of healing work from my childhood. I experienced the finality of the relationship as I'd known it and an extreme loss of hope for what the father-daughter bond could have been. There were missed opportunities, and after his death, there was more healing work to be done. However, making a heartfelt connection with my dad as I became aware of his life-limiting illness made the journey easier.

With my mom, I was several years older when I began to notice her aging.

I suppose for most of us, aging is a gradual process and happens over the years, but as kids, and even adult kids, we often don't see the signs of our parents aging. We don't want to believe it.

I don't think my kids, Michelle and Josh, are particularly aware that I'm aging. I may be deluding myself. They may just kindly ignore my gray hair. I suspect they see me slowing down at times.

Knowing that our days are numbered and life is a precious gift has been my inspiration to make each day count, never hold back, and make the most of my relationships.

After returning to Oklahoma for my mom's ninety-first birthday weekend, thinking this might be my last time to see her alive, she rallied. I then had to make the difficult decision—both personally and professionally—to return home to Portland.

She was still transitional (although the hospice team still hadn't called it) but stable. If that sounds ambiguous, it is. Everything was uncertain. As hard as it was to leave, I flew back to Portland knowing she could die the second I left. I had to trust that whatever happened, the time of her death was out of my hands, and I would be okay.

I returned to Portland on that Monday night, and the very next day, my brother-in-law Dick—my sister Cathy's husband—died. He had been on hospice services with Parkinson's Disease, which is a disease known for its ups and downs, making one's life appear to be nearing death on several occasions but then dying suddenly seeming somewhat unexpected.

Already committed to officiating his funeral, I turned around within two days and flew back to Tulsa. Friday afternoon, after the service when the family gathered, Mom's confusion had visibly increased to the point where she couldn't comprehend Dick's death and didn't recognize her nieces, nephew, daughters, son, or grandkids at various times. This is one common aspect of transitioning.

Something extraordinary was happening; there was a divine force that was pulling on her. She was traveling within different levels of consciousness. Her confusion was real, but things were happening on other spiritual and emotional levels preparing her for her journey. I saw her disconnecting from the world. As a result of the beginning disconnection, confusion can cause discomfort as the dying person tries to understand but can't. This end-of-life experience is also difficult for those around the dying person because they may not be recognized by their loved one.

Even though I knew what was happening and that it was perfectly organic, I felt anxious from anticipatory grief and an awareness of her impending death. The timing of our death is uncertain to us all. It has become clear to me that the timing between each person and their Maker is profound. However, I was deeply aware that the loss of my mom was fairly imminent.

For my sister Cathy, Mom's confusion was excruciating because she couldn't be present for Cathy's deep grief following her husband's death.

On the following Sunday morning, I cried during my morning meditation, releasing the pressure of the cumulative days of intensity with one ear listening for sounds from the other room, anticipating Mom's call as she awakened. In all honesty, I was holding my breath, wondering if she would even wake up that morning. In my journal, I wrote:

Mommy, can you hear me? I love you so much. I'm here,
and I love you. Should I stay with you? Do you want
to be alone with God? I don't have to stay. I know
I can be intense sometimes. I'm such a processor, just like you.
I need to back off. I just love the journey so much.
It seems exciting...and it's in everyone's own time. Stay silent?

Then I received an answer to my questions which gave me peace: "Just be present. Be with yourself, your heart, and Spirit, and just love. You don't have to figure out, fix, or control anything. Love, God."

January 14th was the last entry of that journal. Later that morning, I went for a walk and returned to discover that the assisted living caregivers had already dressed Mom and then situated her in her chair.

The caregivers were notorious for putting her back in her chair when she might've been happier staying in bed.

Mom looked at me and asked, "Why aren't you in school?"

I saw that she was soul-traveling again and asked her, "Mom, how old do you think I am?"

She answered, "Twelve..." Then paused for a moment giving me a puzzling look, she said, "That's not right, is it?"

I smiled, shaking my head no, but then gently explained that she was simply experiencing a life review where she was remembering various parts of her life. I reassured her that her body was doing exactly what it was supposed to do and that everything was just fine.

I saw Mom changing even more. I could no longer assist her to the bathroom. Her body was too weak to engage her muscles—even with her walker, I couldn't do it.

I requested caregiver assistance to put her in her hospital bed. Sitting up took too much effort. She needed to be where she would be most comfortable and exert the least amount of energy. I also requested a hospice nurse visit for later that day to further assess her decline.

While sitting with my mom while she napped, I thought, *Mom's dying, and no one is talking about it.*

In this quiet, reflective time, I was very aware that something was happening here in this profound liminal space between both worlds—physical and spiritual. My attention was immediately drawn to the Hebrew name for the divine feminine presence of God—Shechinah. In this sacred time, everything is interconnected. I consider, death is a natural divine course, and everyone has their own specific time. The dying experience is holy, inviting many spiritual revelations to be with us.

Dying will happen exactly as it's supposed to and, in most circumstances, cannot be rushed.

Later that afternoon, when our hospice nurse, Kris, came, we got Mom back into her hospital bed. Mom's bed became her happy place. She no longer had to work so hard.

Mom thanked Kris and told her how much she meant to her. Patients often thank those caring for them as they get closer to the end of life.

Kris declared Mom was transitioning.

From morning to evening, a person can change so quickly. I called my sisters, Cathy and Cheri, on the phone so that Kris could explain what she was now observing from a medical viewpoint. Mom had been spiritually transitioning for a while, and now the hospice team was assessing her as *physically* transitioning—with her heart fluttering, dis-tinctive gaze, change in complexion, and a decreased desire to get out of bed.

Mom told Kris and me, "I'm right where I'm supposed to be; it's gonna be big." Kris and I looked right at each other with a keen understanding of this common occurrence in hospice nearing the end of life. We both felt Mom was acknowledging her big spiritual journey ahead with acceptance.

I encouraged my sisters to come to Mom's apartment that night. I picked up Cathy, and Cheri and my brother-in-law Michael came in from Oklahoma City. Although Mom was approaching death, she was very lucid that night, actually clear as a bell, so it was important for them to be with her in this vital window.

That night was incredible. I saw Cathy break down in tears as she told Mom that Dick had died. Mom was able to comfort her.

Then Cheri knelt at her bedside in tears and Mom asked, "What's wrong, Baby?"

Cheri answered, "I don't want you to die."

Our mom responded with perfect clarity, attempting to comfort Cheri, "I'm not going anywhere. I'll always be with you."

Revisiting that time as I write this book, I smile and giggle. It was a quintessential moment of a mom's true love and devotion to her children, trying to reassure them—yet one more time, no matter how unrealistic it is—that she wasn't going anywhere and would always be here, even in her dying days.

To me, it was beautiful, and oddly, a moment of reconciliation for Cheri and Mom. Cathy even told me that the only thing Cheri remembers is that Mom would always be with her, and Cheri has felt Mom's presence with her since her death.

That next morning in my new journal, I wrote:

This new journal is dedicated to my mom, Cecile Rose Orenstein Kass Jefferson. Fruitful Lives. A Journey of Blossoming. Passing the Torch. New Beginnings. A Life Well-Lived. Exuberance and Joy. For the Jewels in Her Crown. January 15, 2018.

Mom always identified her three girls as the jewels in her crown—her most precious treasures.

I further wrote in my journal:

Seeing Mom in this state was amazing, beautiful, and incredible. Of course, I had seen this with others, but this was my mom. It brought me such joy. That seems so odd in a way because I was losing my mom. But I wasn't. She was proving, reaffirming, and demonstrating the incredible circle of life—a life well-lived—and the Spirit of God that runs in and through every thread of life. She's shown me Love—big, endless, and overflowing.

In my earlier challenging years with Mom, I honestly wondered how I would feel at the time of her death. Fortunately, she lived long enough for us to grow past our difficulties and respect each other's differences.

Mom's memory loss helped too. We never stopped trying to communicate better. I often challenged her odd comments and worked diligently to figure out the events that triggered her words and thoughts.

My sisters and I had a plan for Mom's care as she approached her last days. We chose a beautiful nonprofit end-of-life home in her community—aesthetically attractive with loving souls who provide impeccable care and a gracious presence. There aren't many of these places around anymore. A person may move in within the last thirty days of life.

We arranged to transport Mom at midday on a Monday. When I woke up that morning, the thought popped into my head that Mom would die on Thursday—in just three days. This was not, at all, related to my professional assessment, I think it was a message from God.

I had planned to return to Portland on Tuesday, the very next day. With that intuitive hit coming into my consciousness, but in truth, Mom's days were still uncertain, I had to see what showed up to guide me in these days ahead.

After getting Mom settled into her new bed at the hospice house, she said to me, "Don't go."

Uncertain what she meant, I asked, "You mean don't go out to the car yet to get the rest of our things?"

Again, she said, "Don't go!"

Realizing that Mom may have remembered from her lucid period Sunday night, it clicked to ask, "You mean don't go back to Portland?"

She nodded and softly answered, "Yes."

I quickly answered and said, "Oh, okay. Give me a minute while I call my boss."

I left for about five minutes and returned with a prompt, "Done." I could feel Mom's energy relax. To be that attuned and connected to recognize her communication and bring her such comfort was incredible.

Serving as a hospice chaplain for many years, I've witnessed a lot of people transition from a physical state into an unknown spiritual consciousness—from this world to the next—which is truly beyond our comprehension.

I have often shared with patient's families that as the body declines and the soul prepares to take flight, the dying person becomes unsettled, anxious, and sometimes agitated. This experience can seem disconcerting and uncomfortable. Sometimes patients have expressed a sense of floating or falling. The human spirit, or the soul, is beginning to disconnect from the physical world.

When my patients would try to explain what they felt and couldn't quite get the right words, I would ask, "Do you feel a little ungrounded?" They usually agreed with that description. I can then explain to them what it seems like may be happening and why, based on my experience with many others. The soul begins to shift and shake loose from the body as it prepares for departure.

On Tuesday evening, Mom was very restless and beginning to get a little agitated. My sister Cathy had already gone home for the evening, and I was staying in the room with Mom.

Every time I did anything, Mom would startle. Over the years, Mom had significant hearing loss, had adamantly refused a hearing aid, and often had to ask what we said. That night, as she was moving into an actively dying state, Mom heard every little sound I made—even crinkle of the paper. Her spiritual hearing had activated.

After about the third or fourth time, I turned to Mom and asked, "Mom, are you wondering what's happening to you?"

Mom nodded her head yes. She really couldn't talk anymore.

"Do you want me to explain what's happening to you right now?" I asked.

She moaned, "Uh-huh."

I took a deep breath and sat at the bedside holding my mom's hand and said, "Mom, you're dying. Your body is dying, but your spirit will live on. It's going to take a little time. You might feel like you're falling; you might feel like you're floating, but you're not. And when God says it's time, all you have to do is relax into God's arms. Everything is happening just as it's supposed to happen." I placed pillows next to her to help her feel safe, secure, and cozy. I could feel my mom's energy settle and release with each breath.

Often when I mention hospice, my work with the dying, and preparation for the end of life, people immediately tell me about their final arrangements. They may have bought a burial plot, a crypt, or a mausoleum space at their local cemetery, arranged for cremation, and finalized their financial obligations for mortuary services. Sometimes, folks offer that they have declared their wishes for specific funeral music.

As a hospice chaplain, I view end-of-life planning as more about the care and attention for the human spirit and the strength of connection within a person's important relationships. I describe this preparation as getting your soul affairs in order. In all candor, tending to the garden of the soul is a lifelong process rather than simply for those who are dying.

Contemplating the anticipated death of my mom and addressing my anticipatory grief helped me share my heartfelt feelings with her before she died.

Often, people wait until a family member becomes ill and at the end of life before they share treasured words such as "I love you," "You mean so much to me," "I'll miss you," "Thank you," or "I am sorry."

If you are harboring discord or resentment, find the place inside of yourself that is hurt, discover why, and seek healing.

Don't wait. Life is short, and we need to make the most of it.

I love working with death, dying, grief, and loss, as it constantly reminds me that life is fragile, and our time together is sacred.

Often, when a person comes to mind, I call or send them a text. These little moments of enlightenment are purposeful. I value my relationships deeply and resolve disturbances quickly to be more available for richer engagement.

As long as we are alive, there will always be spiritual growth and transformation available. Accepting and honoring the soul's journey and its need for continued attention respects the organic nature of life's imperfect spiritual evolution and allows us to enjoy the path rather than be focused on the outcome. Rather than seeking perfection, we acknowledge our progress along the way.

Each person identifies their Maker in different terms—some may personify the divine in literal ways, some may visualize images of nature, and others may. The important thing is not the words, but an awareness and connection to a divine presence as each individual resonates and trusts in their spirit.

The bedside of a dying person is *not* the time to encourage a certain theology. The dying process is a sacred time to honor an individual's holy journey with their Divine Source. I cannot emphasize this enough. This sacred time is about the dying person, their faith and beliefs that support their journey into the unknown, and the inner experience of those loved ones in their presence.

Mom could relax and allow the evolving spiritual process to continue with greater ease.

It was two more days before she passed. During that time, her physical body continued to decline with sounds but no speech, an increase in fluid in her lungs, some labored breathing, and varied moments of lucidity—consciousness. Each time she went into an altered consciousness, she would soul travel. She had a glazed look, and if you were standing in front of her, it appeared that she was looking right past you, no longer making eye contact. She was looking beyond this world.

On previous occasions, when I would ask Mom if she had any wishes, she expressed wanting to see her brothers and parents again. At the time, she wasn't thinking of an afterlife or contemplating the soul's continuation. Mom never thought it would be possible to see her folks or brothers again.

I remember tossing out that rhetorical question in earlier conversations, "What if you could see them again?" She thought that would be nice but didn't think it was possible.

In these last days, she stared off into the distance, even reaching upward and appearing as though she were seeing and connecting with something or someone. Often, people will see loved ones who have already crossed over to the heavenly realm.

Mom focused on the upper right corner of the room. Interestingly, for most of my dying patients, these gazes are in the right corner of the room. I've thought the upper right corner may have something to do with God drawing us toward the Divine realm.

In Judaism, we are instructed to use our right hand for many religious rituals, and in the Torah (the first five books of the Hebrew Bible), several places mention the right hand or the right side. The right is considered the more prestigious one.

In the book of Genesis, Chapter 48, verses 18-19, Jacob insists on placing his right hand on the head of Ephraim while blessing him because of his tribe's future greatness. When holding the Torah, we hold and carry it against the right side of our body. The Mezuzah is a parchment affixed to the right doorpost of a Jewish home inscribed with Hebrew verses from the Torah (Deuteronomy 6:4-9), consisting of the Jewish declaration of faith (Shema Yisrael), acknowledging the oneness of God.

In Jewish mysticism, Kabbalah, the right side of the body houses chochmah (wisdom), chesed (loving-kindness), and netzach (endurance or victory). All of these right-sided awareness guides us to the power, strength and honor of Divine Presence and reminds us that God is in the shadows on our right side for protection.

Intriguingly and mysteriously, these common occurrences often hold a deeper meaning and purpose that beautifully align with the unexplainable holy transformation at the end of life. I believe that in this divine orchestration, Mom's wishes were granted and she did see her brothers and parents, which gave her comfort in her dying journey.

My sisters and I spent that Wednesday night with Mom. It was a restless night for all.

Mom had to be turned every couple of hours, and with so much fluid in her lungs, was quite noisy. She would moan intermittently, seemingly with physical pain. Sounds and noises are not necessarily a bad thing. More likely, these can be expressions of what I would define as spiritual pain. The discomfort, restlessness, and agitation of a dying person have often revealed one's wrestling with their soul's departure from the body, and often indicates a person's review of their life experience. Although Mom was on medications to open her airway and ease her discomfort, her soul's wrestling was apparent.

Mom stirred a bit in those last days as she processed her end-of-life review, but with relative ease, which indicated to me that she had made peace with her life challenges. We had a lot of conversations that I believe helped her explore her life experiences and facilitated an easier, peaceful death.

With most hospice patients, dying is a gradual process rather than an acute event. Often, families feel that their loved ones are lingering in pain, but the length of time it takes for death to occur is purposeful. This period is perfectly divine for the patient and the family to process their loved one's end of life and begin to grieve the relationship.

At one point, around five in the morning, Mom's breathing became rapid and labored. I woke my sisters and told them she may be getting closer to her end. After more medication and just sitting with her, Mom's breathing relaxed, and she settled down again.

I have often identified myself as a midwife to the dying (now known as a death doula). The labored breathing that accompanies an actively dying person is akin to contractions for birthing a child. There are often multiple series of labored breathing with periods of relaxed intervals. Whereas contractions move the birthing process along, preparing the body for delivering a baby, the labored breathing at the end of life seems to help the body prepare for the soul to take flight.

Mom continued to rest with a fair amount of ease.

The biblical figure, Job, had patience with his inner turmoil because of his faith. Through all his lamenting of the suffering he felt, he kept showing up for the process to unfold. He had a strong belief in God.

In the Book of Job, he complained to God about his struggles with his lot in life, wishing some of his journey had been easier. Mom, too, complained and yet rarely mentioned God. However, in some mysterious way, she had faith in a profound power deep within her soul, which instilled gratitude for life itself, appreciation of the world around her, humanity as a whole, resilience beyond all adversity, and trust in her inner strength.

As I have told my children and others as they became Bar and Bat Mitzvah age (thirteen and twelve, respectively), we rise within ourselves. Through the process of becoming, we grow taller inside our spirit.

Is the energy stirring inside anxiety or inner fire? I have often felt that fear, anxiety, excitement, and enthusiasm are all on the same line of energy. Our interpretation and the meaning we assign to the experiences delineate the difference.

Anxiety is uncomfortable for most of us. However, those so-called positive feelings of excitement and enthusiasm can also feel disconcerting if we don't know how to channel the emotion—energy in motion.

Serena Dyer's song "Don't Die With Your Music Still In You" gives us the directive to embrace the vibrant energy of our inner fire, our divine life force, to live out the music in our hearts, and be the people we're meant to be.

One of my seminary professors shared a story about his dear friend and great Jewish Folk singer, Debbie Freidman, before she died. He shared that although Debbie was ill, she was driven to keep writing songs as long as lyrics were channeled through her heart and soul.

I found myself wondering even at that time if she had an inner sense that her time on Earth in her physical body was limited, and she felt compelled to push herself while she was still inspired.

Debbie Freidman has been a Jewish icon in my Jewish music world since one of her earliest performances. I was only fourteen, so she must have been around twenty-four. I remember being mesmerized and enthralled by her spirited energy. I wonder today if she felt anxious in her creative process as she came into her moxie—repeatedly.

Still today, I am in awe of Debbie Friedman's contribution and her vibrant spiritual presence. The voices of the prophets and our ancestors reverberate throughout time. The energy of our loved ones and influential people who have walked this planet before us instills power and inspiration within us, and that sensational drive propels us confidently into our heartfelt dreams. Having the capacity to hold and channel this powerful energy is a gift to be embraced and nourished.

I first became interested and intrigued with death after being with my stepdad, Jeff, when he died. I was at his bedside as he took his last breaths. I felt Jeff's presence. His energy continues with me.

Being with Jeff when he died was only my second experience with a dying person. This was probably my first spiritual experience. I felt something bigger than life itself, and it was indescribably impactful. Holding Jeff's hand at the time of his death spiritually enthralled me as I felt an energy run through me.

Mom and Jeff began their life together when I was in my early teens—you know that time when teenagers think they know everything and need to have the last word. Well, that was me. Jeff and I had wrestled through a few rounds over the years. Looking back, I was struggling with myself, and he watched, and honestly was present with me in a way I'd never experienced. Ultimately, I realized that he was willing to go to the ends of the earth for me.

Jeff had become an integral part of my life for fifteen years. He had lovingly surfed the waves of my teenage and early adulthood emotional turmoil, and then some, and he loved me wholeheartedly.

At the end of Jeff's life, he was breathing on a ventilator and unable to speak. In the palpable silence and inside my heart, I told him that I no longer needed to have the last word.

Although I didn't have words to articulate such an experience at the time, I felt what I would now identify as an energetic hug. Fittingly, Jeff and I had a well-established ritual that was initiated by those car signs people would hang in their car windows that read, "Have you hugged your kid today?"

The grief intensity and the spiritual awareness I felt prompted me to further explore death and learn about what happens when we die.

My cousin Bonnie introduced me to a book called *There Is No Death* by Betty Bethards. Although I don't remember much of the book's details, I remember the title and the comfort it gave me knowing that death is not the end. This powerful statement came well before I learned that we are souls first and then receive a body that houses our souls.

Later, even after attending seminary, I heard a rabbi specifically note that our bodies die but our soul continues. Our soul lives on. We continue in some way, shape, or form.

I was attuned to the presence and energy of deceased spirits at a very early age. I was told both by my mom and then by my sister, Cathy, that at around twelve years old when my grannie died and we arrived at the cemetery, I walked right over to my grandfather Samuel's grave, and in alignment with traditional Jewish practice, I placed a pebble on his marker. I never met either one of my grandfathers and had never been to that cemetery.

Unfortunately, I didn't know what to do with this gift of spiritual attunement for a long time.

Spirituality provides a vast array of possibilities to experience the mystery—the ineffable, intangible, unseen, and unexplainable opportunities that await us in the transformation of the soul.

Death is an organic part of life. It occurs acutely or organically. One may have a dramatic event such as a heart attack, a tragic car accident, or another trauma. Life can end with an illness that ceases to respond to curative treatment or the natural aging process where the body's internal systems no longer function as they once did. Regardless of the way we die, our physical body's existence will end on this Earth.

Like the soul, the body's journey is also a mystery. We can treat our bodies well, provide the best care for our sacred systems, and the body will still die. The duration for each of us is unpredictable. Focusing on the soul's journey, living each day to the fullest, and making each moment matter as our credo, can offer grace and wisdom along this unknown journey.

I've often told my patients' families not to be afraid to talk about death, dying, grief, and loss. These are courageous and sacred conversations. Many families would tell me they were afraid that mentioning death would scare their loved ones.

I can assure you that your aging parent or loved one with an illness has contemplated death and dying on some level. We give our loved ones a sacred gift by talking about death, sharing how we'll feel without them, and anticipating the unknown experience ahead.

Until death is discussed, it is the proverbial elephant in the living room, and everyone holds their breath walking around the house. We can release and mention death and dying. When we breathe more deeply and fully into these vulnerable conversations, we discover common realizations that the death experience—what happens to our bodies and souls at life's end—is unknown. We all ponder the mysterious mystical journey. Sometimes we even engage in the possibilities of how our dying loved one will let us know their spirit is around us.

As a person declines and we share the uncertainties ahead, we often relax and find humor. I used to remind my mom that she'd be able to talk to me and that I'd be looking for the special ways she would show me her presence. Overall I think it gave her comfort.

One of my patients told her son, with immense joy and laughter, that she would kick him in the behind to keep him in line. She loved him so much, hated to be leaving him, worried about him, and had great sadness and grief knowing that she'd leaving him be departing from him.

Talking about the changes ahead and the possibilities of knowing another's presence after death helps to ease the dying person's way. We can ponder more easily the inevitable transition and incredible transformation of life and love that is to come.

Shonda Rhimes, author of *Grey's Anatomy*, wrote about the magical hum of life. "The hum is action and activity…music…light and air, the hum is God's whisper right in my ear…a very magical secret…it's just love."

My mom seems to get my attention with the visits of hummingbirds. Initially, it was the hum and the clicking of their spinning wings reminding me of my mom tapping her long fingernails on the kitchen table. Still today, hummingbirds visit their feeder regularly on my balcony which makes me feel my mom's presence.

I believe in a universal vibrational force that is often beyond our comprehension. It is our divine programming operating continuously through us. That spiritual hum is frequently in front of us, although we may not be aware of it. "It's just love" doesn't do justice to the divine, loving energy that is inherent within our hearts and souls. That magical hum illuminates the spinning spiritual vortex of life.

Love expressions are the little energy sparks present in our encounters that call attention to sacred connections, guide our conversations, and propel us into our next actions. Love can be present even within conflict as the Divine Spirit nudges us to grow.

Mom always told me and my sisters that we were the jewels in her crown. She meant that we were her pride and joy—her greatest accomplishments.

It's quite nice, I suppose, but I cringed a bit and questioned, "I'm an accomplishment or her pride?"

Elizabeth Gilbert states, "The universe buries strange jewels deep within us all and then stands back to see if we can find them."

My mom lived long enough to see her girls discover their gems and thrive. I suspect what made her the proudest was that we found our treasures within ourselves.

Children often display similarities to their parents in behavior and thought. These similarities are transmitted by our loved ones' spirits. They connect us energetically to our ancestral lineage throughout generations. Mom's feistiness energized me. In turn, my husband and I have empowered our children with our family's vibrant spiritual aspects.

I cherish my children's independent journeys, knowing that their internal divine power is forging their path ahead.

Each of us develops mysteriously what we need at just the right time—a new spark of energy arrives within each phase of our journey. In Judaism, we say, "Go from strength to strength"—may our individual and collective inner strength carry us and guide us in every endeavor throughout our lives.

Chapter 6

CONNECTING WITH SPIRITUAL WISDOM

"Grief never ends…but it changes. It's a passage, not a place to stay. Grief is not a sign of weakness, nor a lack of faith…It is the price of love."

—Unknown

For this book, I'm introducing you to the ways we can become further enlightened, living through the layers of loss. This moxie energy comes in spurts that guide and inspire. These divine currents of power and strength can replace our confusion with clarity, comfort, and confidence.

I've created steppingstones for how one may experience moxie surges and shifts that elevate our consciousness. To help you understand these nonlinear, nonspecific facets of the grief journey that are infused with potential moxie energy, I've named them Moxie's Five Initiations: Arriving, Awakening, Accepting, Aligning, and Acting. These are phases of conscious progression that resonate within and enlighten our hearts and souls while moving through loss. Functioning as a personification of divine energy, Moxie Initiations are like archetypes or containers of potential energy that hold the mysteriously creative flow that carries us and guides us through our grief journey. This creative energy is a source of life and love that is ignited within us again and again, and often born through struggle—much like the metamorphis from a caterpillar into a butterfly. These vessels of sacred life force infuse every aspect of our lives.

Although you may not need a structure or a way to label segments of your experiences, these identifications offer a possible framework that can assist with understanding the mystical phases of healing loss. As we travel the layers of loss in our lives, these initiations will invariably cycle and repeat with no apparent order, rhyme, or reason. This is the epitome of the grief process throughout a lifetime. Embracing the transformation over the time of the grief journey needs gentle commitment, loving patience, and gracious openness. The further expansion of this growth process is coming to know in a variety of ways that your deceased loved one's presence is with you. An internal spiritual vibration channels through us and reveals little—and sometimes big—messages to us through emotion, sensations, thought, and vision.

I've described moxie throughout this book as an energy or force that is within and around us. This vigorous influence propels and guides us through this painful grief revealing the various paths forward. With that, how moxie shows up can vary greatly. The progression of these initiations describes how my grief experience awakened me to a stronger sense of Divine Presence and my mom's spiritual essence. Both of these energetic experiences gently pushed me further me on my spiritual transformation, sometimes painful, and at times, joyful.

Diving into the internal angst of grief means embracing all the discomfort and messiness as a way to navigate peaks and valleys that reveal messages from our loved ones clarifying many aspects of our relationship which offer us greater understanding and awareness. The Moxie Initiations are a series of identifiers that explain what any one of us can be experiencing as emotions arise.

Arriving is like a knock on the door—an unexpected arrival of a package or a surprise visitor. Something may startle you to get your attention.

You may meet a person who reminds you of your loved one or see a shirt label or a food package with their name on it like I did. One day I was going about my business doing my grocery shopping and all of a sudden, I was shocked to see my mom's name on a brand label, Cece's Veggie Co, in the health food store. It completely stunned me and got my attention because Mom's name is unique, and she was not a health food shopper.

Awakening triggers inner turmoil that grabs our attention. Something surprises us like a lightning bolt or an electrical current throughout our body, such as seeing a shadow, sense a unique smell, a song out of the blue, or picture that reminds us of our loved one. You might even feel a shiver of grief throughout your entire body. We feel the absence of our person deep within us and long for their presence, we can feel disconnected and yet connected simultaneously. It may even be that first instinctual tug of wanting to call your mom or your spouse when something happens that brings them into your consciousness.

This internal stirring can cause confusion, disbelief, and questioning. This inner awareness encourages an inquiry into the mysterious indications of a loved one's spiritual presence. We might ask ourselves, "Why is this happening? Is Mom really here? Do I really need to feel more sadness, more tears? Is Dad really talking to me? Are these nudges within me from God?" Wrestling with emotional imbalance is uncomfortable. Our inner spirit is awakening and calling on us to look deeper into our essential soul lessons.

Accepting is dropping into the strength and power in honoring exactly where we are at any given moment within our grief journey. This allows us to relax into the multidimensional layered experience of grief. We can then more deeply process our loved one's absence and that life as we've known it has and will continue to change. As I've mentioned earlier, we transition in our relationship to our dear one. We can no longer reach out to them face-to-face, so we become aware of our inner and outer experiences that create a new connection and consciousness within our hearts. As we reestablish our bond, we can then entertain the idea that the soul essence of our deceased loved ones can be present. Attuning to the spiritual messages within our environment can bring great comfort.

The Accepting moxie process truly occurs when a person recognizes the visits of a loved one's presence and invites sacred engagement.

Initially, seeing a hummingbird didn't mean so much. Now every time I speak with my sisters—in person, by phone, or video—and we mention our mom, hummingbirds hover on my balcony, outside my windows, and at their feeder.

For years, thoughts of my dad have come to my mind each time I've seen a white butterfly. I feel strength and wisdom from both my parents at these times, and I believe my awareness of their spiritual presence guides and teaches me more about life and death.

Aligning is when you openly welcome these experiences, believe in their value, and trust the information and insight that comes. There's something bigger than the human condition going on at this point during your grief; it's purposeful and is a unification with the Divine. During this transformation, I began to feel a different energy and then aligned with its powerful presence, which enabled me to trust the divine flow of the Universe. Mom's spiritual presence confirmed the continuation of her soul's existence in these mysterious signs such as hummingbirds visiting me regularly and hearing myself use my mother's words with an energy that is palpable in my thoughts, feelings, and experiences. Recognizing these instances as potent material for remembrance integrates her life force into my heart and home.

Acting with moxie is engaging in new actions that are completely out of our comfort zone and often frightening. Taking action while grieving is difficult and can be daunting. This unexpected new energy inspires us even while we're still in sorrow. Both can be present simultaneously. This energetic movement tugged on my heart and strengthened my faith. These powerful surges became my fuel. Writing this book has been a direct result of this vibrant, mysterious empowering force. In my search for help for my own grief process, asking rabbis for material on the spiritual transformation that's possible through grief, and getting nowhere, I felt an intense guiding force telling me to use my experience—my pain and inner turmoil—to do something good in the world. This is what it means when we say, "May their memory be for a blessing."

I realize today while writing that my mom's persuasive enthusiasm—sometimes annoying and at times, delightfully contagious—was her divinity trying to reach me. I only began to listen more closely in Mom's last few years and now, after her death.

It is valuable to note at this point that the information that describes the experiential nature, purpose, and value of the grief journey was not out in the world. This endeavor of writing a book was the direct result of lived experience and, in many ways, building the plane while flying it. The words to illustrate and offer context to make sense of the unfolding layers connected to loss came much later.

Acting with moxie means courageously embracing the deeply painful emotions of loss. In the process, we find meaning in our loved one's life and their death. We understand ourselves and our loved ones better, cultivating the value of the grief journey emerging from the deep abyss and into the beyond. Acting with moxie means boldly and vulnerably accepting and embracing everlasting love. Openly exploring my emotional responses to my mom's actions in our relationship, healing the pain of loss, and harvesting its precious gems helped me to embrace the richness of life and all its lessons.

Being a hospice chaplain, I am a huge advocate for hospice care. Not all hospices are the same. When someone is in their last phase of life and no longer wishes to have treatment for an illness and is declining, it may be time for a hospice evaluation.

Currently, Medicare governs hospice care, and there are many reasons a person may qualify for hospice. According to Medicare requirements and eligibility, a doctor has to verify that, based on the trajectory of one's illness, they *could* die in six months or less. With that said the effect of hospice care is honestly paradoxical. An individual often lives longer than expected because of the higher level of multidisciplinary care—medical and psycho-social-spiritual care—that addresses and embraces all aspects of a person, their life experiences, and their entire family.

From 2015 to 2017, my mom was evaluated for hospice twice before she became eligible. At these times of evaluation, Mom's demeanor was changing, and although she wasn't near death in these periods, she would've benefitted from hospice care psychologically, socially, and spiritually. She was beginning to withdraw, isolate, and retreat into her own world. Mom's hearing had diminished, she wasn't tracking conversations as well, and didn't want to engage as often so she was staying in her apartment more avoiding community meals in their dining room. As I observed and listened to her, she seemed to be contemplating her inner changes, often revisiting earlier life encounters, and going inward to reconcile her life experiences.

In 2017, a year before she died, Mom admitted that she would benefit by discussing her aging along with her thoughts and beliefs about the end of life. Thinking about what a hospice team can offer, I suggested talking with a social worker, and she liked the idea of sharing the joy of her life experiences. However, medically, her body hadn't declined to the point of hospice acceptance.

Gaining greater awareness of a person's hospice readiness is valuable as we watch our loved ones age and change. I teach and guide individuals and families to recognize these changes and facilitate helpful dialogue before it's time for hospice. Greater attention, care, and conversation is needed for those in the period between the onset of illness and increased signs of aging...before we approach end of life. Becoming more equipped to embrace these psychological, social, and spiritual changes will ease the transition through hospice care.

In my six-month transformational program for individuals and families called *ReSOULution: Sacred Conversations and Connections From Diagnosis Through Grief, Death, and Beyond*, we address the many elements and facets from a diagnosis through the changes towards the end of life, and the many layers of grief during one's decline, within their family relationships to facilitate connection, healing, and transformation during and beyond a death. Grief is complex and multidimensional, and often accumulated with years of unresolved hurt that needs to be resolved.

Engaging in sacred conversations to discuss topics of death, dying, grief, and loss can be quite tricky. There are beautiful organic openings for profound and meaningful discussions. Here's one example of an opportunity with my mom:

Mom: My body just doesn't work the way it used to. (*frustrated*) I also don't remember much at all. I'm sorry. I just forget.

Candi: It's okay, Mom. Your body's doing exactly what it's supposed to do at this age. We know you're in your last phase of life, and things don't work the same.

Mom: Oh. I guess that makes sense.

Candi: What do you think about that?

Mom: You mean this being my last part of life?

Candi: What do you think happens when we die?

These types of chats offer an exchange for a gentle dance to engage with the topics and ease your loved one's frustration about their decline. They are comforted by your acceptance and acknowledgment of their reality. You can deepen the dialogue by expressing your grief by showing your awareness of their future loss.

Building bridges within families by discussing life transitions and fears of death and dying will enliven and enhance the experiences of those in their last phase of life. These are not morbid discussions. They are life-affirming sacred conversations—honoring and revering life. Within this journey, we deepen our connections.

How do we step outside of the mold that someone else designed for us and walk in our truth?

Mom fell in December of 2017, and I knew this was a sign of further decline. Her confusion increased, and she now had more pain. This pain was different. I'd often seen this type of pain with my hospice patients. This was spiritual pain.

The experience of one's internal shifting is sometimes extremely vulnerable. There seems to be an awareness of internal changes laden with strong sensations

of being untethered and uncertain of what's ahead.
My patients would often confirm that
their foundation is shifting.

After Mom's fall, she began to shift dramatically. I could hear her discomfort and uncertainty on the phone and knew it was time for a new hospice evaluation. I reassured my mom that her body was changing now, and everything was okay.

I was on the phone regularly with my sister, Cathy, as our mother's condition was different every day. She arranged Mom's hospice evaluation, and I was able to participate long distance.

Mom was doing what I call life review and soul travel. She would see things that we did not see and blurt out seemingly nonsensical, random comments. I am certain that somewhere inside of her, these sightings and experiences were purposeful for her spiritual journey.

Mom was admitted into hospice care with a wonderful Tulsa hospice team. I could see her beginning to transition spiritually, but medically, her physical body had not yet shifted into a transitional state.

My mom's experience of coming into hospice care close to the end of life is very common. Sometimes the lateness is due to not yet being medically eligible, and at times, it is because many people feel they would be giving up. Sadly, often by the time someone is medically eligible for hospice care, they aren't always able to discuss their mental, emotional, social, and spiritual changes occurring in conjunction with the physical ones. Most folks are contemplating death, dying, grief, and loss at some point during their life as well as at the end of life. Sacred conversations to openly discuss these topics can create rich engagement, deeper connection, and genuine trust (along with a bit of humor!) for the journey ahead with their families and with the care team.

As a hospice chaplain, being present while patients share their realizations and life stories often provides insights into our life journey. To attune to divine inspiration, we need to leave our agendas and expectations at the door of our visits and enter the sacred allow ourselves to enter an sacred liminal space with an open heart and expanded mind. At these moments, we're invited into deep soul awakening. The spirit is present in the stillness of the moment.

Pain from tragic experiences often clouds our vision. Life brings pain and suffering. We have a choice of how to move forward, either despite our challenges or because of our difficulties.

My path has been the latter. I experienced the challenge, felt the pain, and wanted something different. I wanted to feel more connected, to feel better within myself, and about myself. I didn't know why I felt bad, why I held myself back, and why I hadn't loved myself but knew I wanted something different. My desire has been to awaken and feel something magical—something extraordinary—beyond the deadness and numbness I felt inside.

Dead and numb are not identified as feeling words, more like states of consciousness that call on us to search underneath for emotions. But they indicate a sensation of nothingness. I needed to feel my pain—from the past, in the present, and the angst of whatever may arise in the future—so I could experience the magic and joy available to me.

Allowing myself to experience this empty space, I discovered a sacred magical nothingness. In Jewish mysticism, this enchanting place that can be reached along the soul's journey is called Ein Sof, which translates as "no end" but defines an infinite realm. This transcendent divine opening is beyond earthly existence and allows us to explore extraordinary possibilities. To entertain the potential beyond our everyday consciousness invites us into a realm where new light shines and the eternal existence of the soul resides. What a joyful journey! This is where we awaken to our moxie and discover the divine magic and mystery that already exists within us. We're finding our fire again.

At this point in my life, I've learned (and again have been reminded) to follow my inner fire wherever it takes me. Engaging this sense of my mom's enthusiasm and the spiritual awakening offered within the grief journey reminded me of two phrases, "radical amazement" and "spiritual audacity," from the writings of a great Jewish teacher, Rabbi Abraham Joshua Heschel.

Heschel said, "Our goal should be to live life in radical amazement…get up in the morning and look at the world in a way that takes nothing for granted. Everything is phenomenal; everything is incredible; never treat life casually. To be spiritual is to be amazed."

Seeing the world and our experiences through fresh eyes of wonder and curiosity to ask what's being revealed to us by these encounters is to live life to the fullest, discovering each moment with full amazement. This is not a Pollyanna type of view but rather an opportunity to open to new possibilities and perspectives.

My mom exemplified this enthusiastic spirit. Only a few years before her death did I begin to hear her words differently. It is striking to me that I even recognize the wisdom of her words today. Then after her death and in the depths of my grief, the divine spirit of her enthusiasm became more impactful. Oddly now her words seem to be "inspired by God." Even with grief, there's something to learn, and something available to amaze us. Do we have the audacity to seek these spiritual awakenings?

The other brilliant statement by Heschel is: "Sometimes God knocks me over the head with stuff." To be in awe of the way Spirit gets our attention and assists us in awakening to a sacred presence with a direction or a lesson makes life's transformations challenging. Sometimes it can be an annoying adventure, and at other times oddly comforting, but profoundly compelling and encouraging. When challenges hit, we don't necessarily respond with delight, yet if we're open to this divine alert system, we acknowledge that something bigger than us is trying to get our attention.

When something knocks us over the head, it's as if God is tapping us on the shoulder, saying, "Excuse me. Excuse me, honey, I need you to pay attention right here, right now." Those big jolts are generally illness, death, and grief when we're being asked to look inward, explore our inner landscape, travel through our personal arid desert, and seek guidance towards a promised land.

This energy of enthusiasm, the drive of an inner calling, is the Spirit of moxie, and it accompanies the grief journey. For much of my life, my mom nudged me to take risks, and although it was completely aggravating, she was often on point. Mom would 'strongly encourage' me to take dance and tap lessons, and absolutely loved the dramatic way I sang show tunes like *Mame* and *Fiddler on the Roof.* I'm sure she would've loved it if I'd auditioned for theater. Nevertheless, I still enjoy singing all the time and feel connected to my mom when I do.

Much later, I realized her energy was an attempt to instill strength and determination in me, encouraging me to explore who I was and what I wanted and then to go after my heart's desires. Similarly, this is the unfolding of the grief process as well—nudging us to awaken, feel, grow, learn, and step into a new version of our lives and ourselves.

Having provided spiritual care throughout hospitals, within senior communities, and in hospice for several years, serving those who are aging, and having many conversations about death and dying, I would intentionally engage my mom in pointed, related discussions. Since we were both counselors, we enjoyed the exploration, and Mom would often ask me about my work, which would deepen the talks between us.

Mom and I had common interests and similar frameworks with a different focus but were always intrigued by the emotional process. She was a marriage and family therapist. While I was a chaplain intern at Long Beach Memorial Medical Center, I had long commutes with lots of time to talk to her on the phone.

There were many days when I would have an experience with a patient and a family that touched my heart and reminded me that my mom wouldn't be here forever. I began to call her whenever I thought of her, or the next available segment of time. I would tell her I knew she wouldn't be here forever, pausing at that moment to tell her how much I loved her. I would say thank you for being a good mother, even if there were times I didn't think she was, because I knew I turned out okay. She did a lot of things right, and these were the acknowledgments she needed to make her way toward her life's completion. I never lied or placated (okay, a little placating). If something needed to be said about what didn't go well, I would let her know along with sharing how I healed the hurt.

Since I saw her changing and had experience talking about end-of-life, if it seemed she might benefit, I initiated those conversations as often as possible. Our discussions explored theology, philosophy, and the topics she felt were important, meaningful, and valuable. I found myself listening more intently as if there was a voice of my mom that was new to me and caught my attention more deeply. All of a sudden, I was listening to her words and hearing her in a way I never had.

Recognizing someone's decline lends priceless opportunities. As my mom retreated into silent pondering, she stopped dining with the senior center community and stayed in her apartment. I noticed that she couldn't follow the conversations as easily, which increased her confusion and produced insecurity. She couldn't respond as quickly and zestfully as she once had unless she was well-rested. When she was fatigued, the effort to engage seemed to be too much.

These changes that I am describing gradually occurred over a year.

Although Mom's faculties seemed to be diminishing, she was acting differently and letting go of her regular activities, a new clarity and certainty was arising. I remember feeling something fresh and enlightened in her voice as I discussed with her a new grief group I wanted to facilitate and hearing her emphatically tell me to just do it. That voice came from another place inside her.

Mom used to suggest ideas and would nudge me to oblige. Her energy felt as if she was trying to live out her dreams. But by this time, it was different—her voice became a sort of still, small voice of clear, clean, direct guidance.

The odd and noteworthy part about the grief group conversation was that she remembered it the next time we spoke, even though much of her short-term memory wasn't accessible to her at this point.

Working with many patients in the last phase of their lives, the items that keep surfacing mean something to them. It can be connected to their memories—positive or negative—but a specific event may surface that needs acknowledgment or reconciliation.

In my mom's counseling practice, she also worked with multiple types of losses. My mom and I had similar qualities and skills: a good listener, sharing a depth of wisdom, empathy, and a healthy ability to synthesize a multitude of experiences. We often shared experiences and practices about facilitating groups and working with grief—all of which had been valuable and meaningful contributions to my mom's work life and were pleasant memories to recall. Throughout the years, we would inevitably run into former clients whom she'd helped with their relationships who simply raved about her. Mom saw so much of herself in me that she encouraged me to follow my moxie, use my gifts, and make my own special offerings to the world.

The grief process is near and dear to my heart and holds tremendous value for greater growth, change, and finding our ever-evolving life purpose.

Probably because of my hospice work, I was keenly aware of Mom's emotional and social changes along the way. Each new awareness ...prompted a further opening for significantly deeper dialogue, both for her and for me.

These moments are subtle and easily missed, but if we can pause and deepen the awareness and meaning associated with the occurrences, the opportunities within the change can be nourishing and enlightening. Listening closely to your aging and changing parent, partner, or friend allows you to seize the moment and participate in a richer engagement.

There is often a reason for an odd or off-color remark. I found this to be true as I continued to engage my mom in her last phase of life. For years before this time, I had begun calling Mom out on certain comments she would make if they sounded odd or off. As an example, when I was beginning the entrance process for seminary, I wanted to enter the rabbinical program to become a rabbi.

Becoming a chaplain had always been my desire. I never held an interest in becoming a congregational rabbi, nor did I need to be a rabbi to be a Jewish chaplain. Nevertheless, for broader education and training, the rabbinical program was my initial approach.

My mom asked me, "Why would you want to become a rabbi?"

I was quite taken back and didn't know what to do with that question. I wasn't sure what prompted the inquiry, and I perceived the energy as judgmental. My mom said whatever came to her mind, but this comment struck me as a little more off than usual.

Initially, I felt hurt sitting with my assumption that she thought I wouldn't make a good rabbi and just let it slide.

But she asked again.

I then asked her what prompted her comment.

She said, "Well, it'll take you away from the family, and they need you. Arnie also needs your help."

I paused, thought for a moment, and mentioned that Arnie and I had discussed it. Then a question popped into my mind; "Mom, you mentioned concern about me spending time with the kids and how Arnie might respond to me being away at school. I'm wondering if you were reflecting on your past concerns about me having spent a lot of time alone after you and Dad divorced. I remember you worried about me a lot in those days."

She responded with, "Oh, maybe that's it."

I confessed that I thought she was saying that she didn't think I'd make a good rabbi.

She quickly jumped in telling me that she'd be proud of me no matter what and that I'd be great at whatever I chose to do.

I was relieved.

She realized during our exchange that she must've been processing a significant part of her life. This conversation was the beginning of

Mom's reconciliation with some challenging aspects and experiences in her life —nine years before her death.

We don't need to wait until the last phase of our life to reconcile with our life's challenges.

In 2016, during the last two years of Mom's life, another big noticeable change was that she began to mention God. Until then, Mom's concept of God had been an empowering, positive energy. Her belief system was more like a stance of "I am woman, hear me roar" from the popular Helen Reddy hit song of the 70s. For years, Mom would reference God as "She" instead of "He," implying that women were in charge. At this stage of her life, I experienced my mom's energy differently as these attitudes and interpretations shifted. Mom mentioned God with a sense of comfort, inner certainty, and peace, minus the gender delineation, with a sort of acceptance of her destiny I had never experienced with her before—as if she now knew God in a new way.

In the introduction of *Moxie*, I explored the differences between excitement and enthusiasm and highlighted the Latin root *entheos* for enthusiasm—meaning inspired by God. Something was coming through anew.

My mom and her avoidance of talking about God, consciously or unconsciously, always puzzled me. As I began to develop spiritually and became aware of God's presence, I hoped that she and I could talk about God as a way of connecting more deeply. I was repeatedly frustrated with what seemed like her lack of connection and an insistence that she was in charge. This message created an internal barrier for me and established an idea that I too needed to be in charge rather than trust a higher source.

Later as I unpacked our relationship during my grief journey, I pondered the possibility that maybe her spirited drive was expressing her divinity and devotion to a greater power. Maybe we don't need to talk about God to know Divine Presence and to be driven by our inner inspiration. This is an example of how one can be aligned with a religion—a set of beliefs—and not always be in a relationship with a divine presence which is the essence of spirituality.

This is what chaplains do; we ponder spirituality—all ways of practice and engagement that enliven a human spirit. Divine awakening, a revelation of sacred presence, can arise in a multitude of ways. We are all in various places on our spiritual journey. Our moxie, the Divine Presence within us, and our enthusiasm are the sparks that light up our spirit. What is the energy that brings us alive, ignites our fire, propels us forward, and inspires us to bring our Higher Self to the world?

Our actions and inactions, our beliefs and opinions, our identity and safety, all matter. Of late, our world has been shaken. Divisions—negativity, degradation of self and others, hard stoic stands, attitudes of rightdoing and wrongdoing, yours versus mine, and they versus them—need to stop. We can then rediscover the magic and miracles within each precious soul and all play together.

"Out beyond ideas of wrongdoing and rightdoing,
there's a field. I'll meet you there."

—Rumi, 13th Century Persian Poet

Whether in my personal journey, in my prison work, hospital, or hospice care, over the years in my role as a chaplain and spiritual counselor, I have heard families, friends, clients, and patients express these reactions: "This happened so many years ago." "It's in the past." "I've let that go." "I'm over it." "Forget about it, it's over."

In my case, I needed to discover why I didn't feel like I was enough and tried, repeatedly, to be more. I can't decide your path of healing, nor will I begin to try. However, as a chaplain counseling you with inner challenges, I might pose questions for you to ponder: What might your inner dialogue be saying? What loss might you have buried?

The greatest gnawing pain within my gut was the loss of someone very dear to me, my Self—my authentic self. With a capital S—Source, Spirit, Self—the highest version of ourselves is the divine spark of God. We are direct images of the Divine. On some level, we may know this. However, when we negate ourselves, we create an illusion of separation from Our Creator.

Moxie is the courageous and steadfast engagement with SELF—Source Energy Loving Force—and the world around us. The moxie life force breaks through barriers and opens doors to divine enlightenment, joy, and freedom. Full engagement with what surfaces is the incandescent fuel that propels us forward in life.

Thich Nhat Hanh wrote, "If you look deeply in the palm of your hand, you will see your parents and all generations of your ancestors. All of them are alive at this moment. Each is present in your body. You are the continuation of these people."

Our Divine Creator, God's army of angels, the soul essence of our parents, grandparents, and all of our ancestors, as well as all aspects of nature and inexplicable universal celestial beings, reveal a powerful life force that assists us in allmeasures of our life's journey.

This life force is the moxie energy traveling down through generations. This sacred presence and divine wisdom exist within us and all around us…right in the palm of our hands.

I have an accountability partner who I've renamed an "inspiration partner." The beauty of partnering in life's inspirations and aspirations is helping each other grow to remain on an ever-changing course. Bumps in the road can arise out of nowhere.

When something inside of us is ignited—good, bad, or ugly—we need to search for the meaning inside of ourselves. This is for us and about us and serves to expand our consciousness.

Viktor Frankl, author of *Man's Search for Meaning*, found meaning and purpose while living in the inhumane environments of the Holocaust concentration camps. His suffering called on him to search for the "why"; not "why was this happening," but why he wanted to live. He further discovered the fire in his soul, his moxie, and found purpose in his experience—to survive, reunite with his loved ones, tell what happened, and share what he learned.

Friedrich Nietzsche's quote, "One must have chaos in oneself to give birth to a dancing star," speaks to the value of embracing our inner discord with curiosity and compassion so that we may understand ourselves better and discover our vibrant radiance. These revelations become our greatest gifts, holding the wisdom of life. These precious gems we unearth need to be intentionally polished to shine and reflect our divine light.

Elevating our consciousness on our spiritual path means recognizing that the actual events in our lives may not matter as much as the judgments we make about them. Judgments of ourselves block our life force and dim our inner light. For example, at times during the book writing process, I judged myself. To continue forging the path ahead. I had to clear every judgment that arose because authoring a book requires tremendous emotional and spiritual energy. Forgiving myself and recognizing the value of these lessons cleared the way for me to receive greater inspiration and intuition along the journey.

Ralph Waldo Emerson wrote, "It's not the destination; it's the journey." The journey toward a particular destination is where we often experience challenges. In these times of adversity, we learn the greatest lessons and reap immeasurable rewards.

The process is to navigate the difficulties and discover the purpose in each segment of the journey. Once again, processing loss does not mean remaining in a perpetual state of pain. Although pain is inevitable, facing our emotions associated with life experiences lessens the pain. To heal our hearts requires us to examine our pain connected to our relationships and life encounters. Pain prompts us to explore our inner landscape and connect the dots completing the picture of our lives.

Processing the issues stored beneath my anxiety and self-judgment reveals buried fears and begins to dissolve my protective armor. By clearing my judgments and limiting beliefs, my trust in this divinely inspired co-creative process deepened. Spiritual growth and soul evolution offer us infinite opportunities to discover new awareness and awaken us to divine power. As we walk through our lives, moxie energy guides us at every intersection.

I knew Mom's spirit was somewhere around me, and wanted to know her more in the spiritual realm. I knew it was possible. The silence of her absence was deafening. It felt hollow, empty, and dark. I kept writing and talking to her, and she finally wrote back to me through my hands in my journal. I sensed Mom was affirming that her spirit was near. Then, I heard, "There's just a lot to do when you cross over."

Within my heart, I was giggling and smiling—thankful for Mom's response. That statement sounded so much like words she would have said. I believe that our knowing of a loved one's presence is affirmed when something occurs, or particular words come through that resonate in our consciousness.

A person's spirit can show up in a variety of ways. These sacred encounters are often unexpected taking us by surprise. A loved one may let us know they're near by something we see, feel, smell, or hear. Goose bumps, tears, and bodily sensations are often confirmation of their presence. We might experience a loved one's essence as we see or hear certain words, phrases, and lyrics. These energetic occurrences often bring a sense of comfort. At times, I've felt both my parents and other loved ones guiding and inspiring me.

These spiritual connections are available to all of us. Years ago, after one of my grandmothers died, I smelled her cologne while walking along the sidewalk. It was so strange. I looked around not expecting to see my grandmother but very aware of this real and distinct experience.

One of my clients, Elizabeth, tells the story about a time
a few years following her father-in-law's death
when she and her son were playing on the front porch.
All of sudden, Elizabeth smelled her father-in-law's
Old Spice aftershave. She looked up wondering
why she sensed his presence. Remembering
how much he adored her son, it all became clear.

These experiences remind us that we're always connected. These energetic experiences can be an opportunity to pause, reflect, and create a new relationship with our loved one as well as expand our meaning of life and death.

While visiting a colleague and exploring a new chaplaincy position, I noticed my mom's formal name, Cecile, on a tiny piece of paper. She rarely used this name and it startled me to see it. Shortly after that while in a clothing store, I unexpectedly spotted another version of her name that she didn't like. Mom was letting me know that this wasn't the right position for me. I mentally thanked her and moved on.

Writing letters to Mom, asking her questions, and spending time thinking about her was painful and yet oddly comforting. I heard her somewhere inside myself. Hearing my mom is not the same audible voice that you and I may hear directly from our speech. Sometimes, I hear a word in my mind or have a deep sense of what she's saying. We just know.

One of my grief clients shared with me that she heard her deceased husband whisper, "I'm sorry."

Sometimes, I've heard distinct words that my mom might've said. I've come to acknowledge that voice, enjoy the connections, and welcome. the spiritual communication.

There is some type of holding period, of sorts, after we die. Of course, no one really knows, so we can only speculate according to our belief system and what resonates for us. In seminary, I studied one perspective of a layover en route to our final destination. Pondering what happens during the dying process and after we leave this earth brings me great joy, even makes me laugh at times. Adopting a believable viewpoint about what's to come can be comforting and grounding, and even bring a bit of humor.

I trust the messages I receive. Attuning to our emotional, mental. physical, and spiritual internal messages guides us to discover deep resonance with our hearts and souls. Aligning with our soul's authentic journey is one of the main purposes of *Moxie*.

Before Mom died, I reminded her that she'd be able to "spiritually" talk to me and send me messages from beyond. I don't know how this happens; I just know it does. In those early months after Mom's death, there was an eerie silence when I'd call out to her. After no response from Mom, I called out to Dad, who'd been dead for twenty-three years at that time, to find comfort. Before this time, I had only heard from his spirit once fifteen years before Mom died while I was reading Rabbi Eli Spitz's book, *Does the Soul Survive?* The morning after hearing the rabbi speak, I heard my dad say, "Your sisters need to read this book. Cathy, no problem. Cheri will be a tough nut to crack." This sounded exactly like my dad's.

So, all these years later, I trusted he'd respond to me. When I hadn't heard from Mom's spirit, I asked if he'd seen her and if she was okay.

He told me she would be busy for a while and would be more accessible later.

I listened to Christina Perri's song "A Thousand Years"—easily a thousand times—crying every time. Feeling my emotions is how I connect. Being emotionally vulnerable opens a spiritual pathway for divine guidance to be received. Sometimes, we worry that once we turn on the emotional faucet, the feelings will never stop. Many of us grew up with family messages like "don't cry," insinuating that we were weak. If tears are surfacing, their release is needed for our healing. When we make space for our emotions, honoring the impact of our experiences, we strengthen our resilience.

The pain of my loss from my mom's absence was already with me and was only the beginning. The song helped me access my emotions and transform my pain which then allowed me to feel her presence. Nurturing myself with the permission to feel deeply opened my heart and soul for greater healing. I also felt a new spiritual awareness of my mom. A deep message was being revealed to me within this song.

Perri's song lyrics touched me deeply and gave me greater insight that profoundly changed my life.

"A Thousand Years" was originally written for lovers, but I was embracing the deepest revelation of loving I had ever known. The lyrics ignited my understanding that my mom's love was immeasurable. For many years, because of my early trauma, my mom's love felt too sweet and sticky and risky to trust. I had never known her love in this way. I'd known divine love but never associated it with my mom. Within my broken heart, now open, I knew that Mom's love was God's love, sourced by Spirit—endless, eternal, and everlasting. I now knew that this love was God's love. Mom's love was sourced by Spirit, eternal love that was and is endless and everlasting. Even though more intense, tearful moments would arise, this transformational juncture showed me that Mom's spirit would always be with me.

In contrast, another favorite song ("Someone to Love" by Lukas Graham) warms my heart for my husband, Arnie, Although that love is big, beautiful, and endless, the feeling and depth are very different. Mom had been with me my entire life as I developed throughout life's stages. Arnie and I have grown together over time.

As I played the song identifying it with Mom, I realized she'd loved me for a thousand years and would love me for a thousand more—forever, and areassurance of her undying presence. As I awakened to this deeper understanding and depth of love, I wondered if my children would feel this indescribable loving energy from me one day.

Why don't we know this depth of love? Maybe some of you may do.

The degree of love an individual feels is quite subjective and would be understandably difficult to measure. If we haven't felt this depth of love, then why haven't we allowed ourselves to be loved to this magnitude? I disconnecte d at the time of my parents' divorce, questioned the validity of love, and didn't know how to trust the world. When we face the loss of a relationship either by death or a severed emotional bond, we become aware of the threads of grief that are connected throughout our lives.

In order to be vulnerable and receive such love requires a faith that the love expressed is authentic. I only began to embrace and trust Mom's love later in my life. In my exploration, I discovered her motivation that fueled her actions was love.

Brené Brown boldly says, "Vulnerability is our greatest measure of courage." Interestingly, the root of the word courage is cor, meaning heart in Latin. In earlier times, the word courage meant "to speak one's mind by sharing one's heart." Learning to be vulnerable and to love bravely takes incredible moxie.

In my earlier years, I built a wall of ego, pride, and indignation—my fear, anger, and lack of trust in the world—which hindered my ability to receive the love of this intensity. I knew my mom loved me, but I also believed that she and my life should have been different. These awarenesses were revealed to me over years of healing work.

Following my mom's death within my grief process, both her spiritual presence and my awakening to this new depth of love revealed to me that more love would've been possible throughout our lives together. However, life's events—that create our perceptions, doubts, and fears often block loving connections.

My inner over nearly four decades cleared many hurts and opened my heart which allowed me to reconnect with Mom's love before she died—this infinite, loving consciousness.

Chapter 7

INTERGENERATIONAL PATTERNS

"Exploring our life patterns, healing our hurts, clarifying our misperceptions, releasing judgments, and finding compassion transforms our spiritual injuries and benefits everyone. We expand our spiritual consciousness, discover our soul's wholeness, see with different eyes, and bring light to the world."

—Chaplain Candi Wuhrman

Accepting and exploring my grief through a spiritual lens became the catalyzing transformative journey that allowed my moxie to emerge. Exploring my grief, even fifty years back, has allowed me to understand myself, my family experiences, and my life purpose more clearly. Despite their difficulties, I am certain that my parents and grandparents made the best decisions possible at each juncture of their lives. The choices they made ultimately provided me with opportunities that I couldn't have ever imagined.

Trauma is an event or series of events that can produce spiritual injuries—painful wounds to the human spirit. The cumulative effects of spiritual injuries cause us to recoil from life, squelch our voices, and hide our joyful authentic spirit. Many of us avoid encounters that trigger beliefs that tell us we're not good enough. We've minimized, negated, run from, and pushed away situations that activate those shame-based beliefs. When we share our pain, interpretations, and reactions related to a given experience, we can heal the hurt and begin to live our lives with greater ease and freedom.

When my parents divorced during my childhood, my spirit was devastated. My entire world changed drastically and the trauma of my childhood clouded the filter through which I processed life. For a very long time, I couldn't remember any of my life prior to age nine. My family turmoil was where my story began.

The lasting challenges of this one tangible event resulted in a multitude of elusive, unforeseen effects. I didn't understand life, and didn't know how to cope. I felt abandoned by my dad and blamed myself. Like so many children of divorced parents, I unknowingly established a belief that it was my fault that my parents' marriage dissolved.

The overarching effect was disconnecting from myself emotionally, mentally, physically, and spiritually. I shut off my emotions because I didn't know that feelings were okay. I didn't know that pain was a normal response to such loss and didn't know about grief. I couldn't understand why my family fell apart. Processing information became difficult so I avoided learning opportunities. This may have contributed to my attention-deficit hyperactivity disorder (ADHD). My confusion produced an uncertainty of the world. On a, physical level, I judged my body as inadequate.

At that time, I had no idea I was seeking control within my world. I began using excess food to bury my emotions, to soothe, and fill an emptiness at my core. Spiritually, I'd lost the song and dance within my soul and judged my inner spirit as flawed.

This incomprehe nsible painful loss left me confused and uncertain about family, life, and myself. The pain felt too intense to bear.

Using food to squelch my extreme fear helped me survive, but often anger was expressed as a result of feeling powerless over the circumstances in my life.

Fifty years ago, the impact of my losses from family turmoil, parents' divorce, and multiple moves were never acknowledged. At that time, people hadn't heard of Adverse Childhood Experiences (ACEs), which are traumatic events occurring before eighteen years of age resulting in toxic stress. When intense stressors are unacknowle dged, unrelieved, and unresolved, without support systems to assist in coping, the effects become toxic to the body and brain.

My family did the best they could with what they had, but there weren't adequate resources available at that time.

My dad married my stepmom and moved away while my mom returned to school to become a marriage and family therapist, most likely to help herself and me. She then enrolled me in therapy.

However, none of this was satisfactory. My mom depended on my sister Cheri for many of the household duties, which was overwhelming for her. Cheri had to grow up quickly—from a child one day to living with the expectations of an adult the next. My other sister Cathy was away at college.

I suppose everyone was dealing with our family's dissolution in their own way. Although we were still a family, our interactions changed drastically. Only when writing this book, I became aware that we must've all been grieving to some degree. To share the depth of our pain and connect would've been helpful and nourishing. However, our family had difficulty expressing feelings freely which made it challenging to relate during this loss. There was no guidebook, and none of us knew how to deal with the experience.

My coping mechanism was to push my pain down with whatever was available. Avoidance only postpones the pain. Emotional pain is stored in our bodies and our souls. Connecting with the depth and darkness of my loss made me aware of my lack of connection and became my catalyst for change.

"Spiritual Injuries are the result of traumatic events that hurt our spirit and unknowing ly cause us to ignore our voice, forget our joy, and hide our light." -Chaplain Candi Wuhrman

The effect of these painful spiritual injuries caused me to doubt my worth and hide my divine light.

As grief goes, one loss builds on another. Our discomfort grows and becomes a contributing factor to our uncertainty in life. My family, like many others, is affected by generations of patterns that subtly impact our ability to communicate and cope with challenges. These inherited trauma patterns are cultural, familial, and religious intergenerational influences that have imprinted our spirit and psyche. Many of us are told to maintain composure by controlling our emotions, to push them down in order not to feel to portray a strong image. These messages are often unspoken and modeled establishing expectations within our family systems and cultural traditions.

I was told these types of things for years, even into my adult years. These are not simply our parents' mistakes, but patterns born of generations of our parents, grandparents, and great-grandparents merely following suit. Many of us learned that showing emotion was a sign of weakness and, if expressed, might've been detrimental. Therefore, holding back feelings became a means of survival.

From my perspective, my family had little ability to deal with the heartbreak of the divorce. All that transpired before, during, and following this significant life event ignited fear, doubt, confusion, and anger within my world and all my relationships.

Kids are often viewed as resilient, but they still need help to bounce back, even when they resist it. Children may seem resilient when they're still involved in their daily activities and don't have much to say about their experiences, but that's because they can't yet articulate their feelings. Their wounds remain imprinted within their internal landscape.

Pain is the motivator for us to change.

In my personal story, while seeking comfort and control, I began eating compulsively (around four years old) and later sought other outlets to fill my emptiness. As children, we often learn to compartmentalize to function in life, and for a time, that works. We hide behind a facadé that gives an impression of thriving. We can only uphold these images for short intervals.

As kids, and as adults, we intuitively know what feels good emotionally and spiritually that tells us we're loved and valued. We only learn by the modeling from our parents or family members and within our community. Most children wouldn't have known how to ask for loving presence, reassurance, and safety at the time a trauma occurred nor how to proceed if their family fell apart.

Kids are affected by their environment, the words they hear, and the energy they feel from the circumstances they experience. Layers of confusion and unresolved hurt throughout our lifetime complicates our grief. Questioning whether we were loved and valued makes the grief journey a complex experience to unpack.

With that said, our interpretations, perceptions, understandings, and misunderstandings that we attach to our life experiences set the course for our soul's learning. A painful childhood is not always followed by a problematic adult life. We cannot bypass or bury our turmoil. Our most painful encounters become the steppingsto nes for our greatest learning.

Hanging in my living room is a quote by Jean De La Bruyere, "Out of difficulties grow miracles." The challenges we face in life open our eyes and hearts and connect the fragmented pieces of our lives. There is often a broader understanding and greater purpose beyond our original experiences.

As spiritual beings, our souls are resilient. Our experiences accumulate. As we go about life, the human condition pushes and nudges us to seek help, learn processing practices, and embrace our inner spirit with love.

After a loss, we develop coping mechanisms that can be distractions to minimize our pain. We can only avoid our pain for so long. Our issues will surface at some point.

Unresolved emotional pain can manifest in health challenges, addiction, and poor communication—like anger, edginess, control, and sarcasm. It can also be expressed as discontent within ourselves and then bubble over in our business dealings.

When we shut down our grief, we shut down our light.

All of our unresolved issues affect our human spirit and weigh on our hearts. Addressing them guides us to grow, change, and heal. In turn, we discover contentment, freedom, and inner peace. This unpredictable, imprecise spiritual journey leads us to a greater understanding of the purpose of our life.

It is human nature to avoid discomfort and pain. After attempting to escape my pain through alcohol, food, and hiding, looking for an easier path, I then discovered that facing my difficulties was more valuable than repeatedly sidestepping them.

An elephant in the living room is very difficult to ignore. Elephants are incredible animals; however, one would become hungry, noisy, and quite smelly in the center of our homes. Despite this, we tend to continually walk around that elephant before it gets our attention.

My father, at the age of eleven, escaped Germany during the Nazi regime and the time of the Holocaust with my aunt and grandparents. This makes him a Holocaust survivor, and me, as one of three daughters, a second-generation Holocaust survivor. Dad never spoke of his time in Germany, nor much about his childhood experiences, so I knew very little. He wrote a small book of memoirs very close to the end of his life, where there was only a brief mention of the angst around the trauma in Germany. Up until now, I haven't been able to read the memoirs and had no awareness, other than hearsay, about any of our sacred history to consciously validate how it could have affected me.

In the last several years, I've asked a lot more questions. I suspect, like many others affected, Dad had no words to describe the horrors he saw and felt as his family's world was torn apart simply for their Jewish identity. Until recently, the brief snippets I heard exemplified their remarkable survival. Very little was spoken of the spiritual, psychological, and emotional residue that stores within us. Our ancestors may have come through the physical experience of trauma, but the unidentified remnants are woven into our spirits with unprocessed emotional scars.

I'm certain my dad wanted to protect me. However, learning more about our family history would've explained his way of being and the traits being passed down. Feeling the need to hide and fear of being visible are two significant patterns I inherited from my family history. Intergenerational patterns are transmitted when things are not acknowledged or discussed.

Nearing publication of this book, I received notes from a speech given nearly 70 years ago by my grandmother where she told her story. She explained how the Germans confiscated their home, business, car, jewels, life insurance, and savings. They were allowed to exit the country with only ten dollars to travel to the United States. In the years following, my grandparents established thriving businesses, household, and a life for their family in America. My family history speaks to horrors of an abuse of power, discrimination, and immigration as well as faith, resilience, survival, and developing trust in new possibilities.

The wounds from intergenerational, inherited ethnic, cultural, and family trauma are unknowingly passed onto the next generation. Our ancestors—parents and grandparents—could not have known the potential effects. Our deep-seated fears of living authentically within our ethnic identity can threaten our sense of safety and freedom. My dad never talked to me about his fear and trauma that resulted from his early years in Germany. Those horrific experiences were held viscerally within the cells of his body and spirit. This has influenced my Jewish life as well.

When inequity and indifference exist—spoken, implied, or harbored within us—they form an inner prison that blocks heart-centered connections. We establish internal coping strategies, emotional patterns, and belief systems trying to make sense of the world's injustice to protect ourselves from further harm. Wrestling with going forward, I engage in spirit-to-spirit conversation with my grandmother:

> *Candi:* Nonnie, are you there? How did you avoid shrinking or hiding yourself given what you endured in Germany? I wish I could ask you now in person. I was so scared of your power, strength, and edge when you were alive.
>
> *Nonnie*: Candi, That's how I did it! I drew on that. Just like you're doing now with your moxie. The messaging that we shouldn't exist, have possessions, a voice, and wealth, and in some way were dirty, was so painful. That was sickness. We all deserve to be here. We exist because of God, a Source bigger than us, giving us power, divine power, and strength. Rise with Resilience. That is how we prove that they were wrong. We have a right to live a life of value. Use that power, My Love. Source is bigger than all people.

We can all be divine vessels for change and transformation.

In Mississippi in the early sixties, my dad refused to perpetuate further discrimination when asked as a hospital administrator to build separate entrances—one black, one white. He devised an alternative plan to avoid degrading members of the community. The effects of trauma for individuals, families, and the collective are multilayered and extend broadly. My dad took courageous action to eliminate cruelty to honor all humanity.

Although I've felt the fears channeled down through generations, I've also most certainly drawn on the courage, power, and strength of my ancestors, which has carried me forward in life. My moxie is using that courage to release the fear, blame, and shame of inhumane, brutal treatment by the Nazi regime. Releasing historical burdens and embracing my family's remarkable moxie to survive and thrive allows me to live fully—often fearlessly—to stand tall and proud of my heritage, bravely face injustice, and boldly discuss life and death with others.

I would encourage anyone who feels they've been wronged or experienced injustice to dive deeply into their trauma history to avoid projecting their own internal biases onto others. Projection of individual, unresolved trauma carries forward within families and intensifies collective trauma within our communities. We, as a people, have the courage, power, and strength to heal past hurts, break the cycles of worldly trauma, and create healthier, connected multicultural societies. This is not about using physical force or hierarchy from powerful positions. It's about coming home to ourselves, connecting to our inner awareness, and awakening to the truth of who we are.

Healing individual and family patterns requires an acknowledgment of trauma. As retired physician Gabor Maté explains in his work, trauma does not need to be war, genocide, murder, or extreme acts of physical or sexual abuse. He believes trauma is beneath all human dysfunction. Dysfunction can produce addiction, affliction, confusion, and disease, which causes us to emotionally separate from ourselves. Trauma occurs when a child feels no one is available to hear their pain. Children and adults hide their authentic selves when they don't feel they hold value. Dr. Maté shares in his documentary, *The*

Wisdom of Trauma, that because all trauma is generational and therefore inherited, it's no one's fault.

This can be hard to accept. The energy fueling our anger and resentment seeks to assign blame in an attempt to avoid and bury our deepest hurts. This is one of the ways we hide from our pain. We often feel we need someone, anyone, to take responsibility for inflicted harm. Many of us will experience the effects of traumas throughout our lives from our family, society, politics, and environment, just to name a few. We often minimize that impact in the hope that we can shield ourselves from further injury and harm.

As much as we attempt to bury our trauma—push it aside or mask it—it will resurface. People often proclaim they'll take their secrets to the grave, and yet, I've witnessed many patients whose trauma resurfaced at the end of life. When someone approaches their final days without having addressed their life's trauma unresolved issues will often emerge through significant restlessness and agitation. The discomfort may appear to be physical pain, but it's, in fact, spiritual pain as the soul wrestles with its life experiences. Medication is often prescribed but will not always alleviate the spiritual distress and alternative interventions may be needed. Medication, along with the presence of a chaplain, can facilitate an ease and freedom for their transition.

To lessen such difficulties I recommend ongoing discussions about life's challenges and changes as they arise. By the time someone reaches hospice, they don't have the capacity to process their relationships with the depth needed for complete resolution. In addition to the loss of a person's physical presence following a death, their unresolved emotional pain and trauma can leave unexpected burdens on their family. This is a common occurrence and often unavoidable. Your loved one's unaddress ed pain may have little to do with you, but you may feel its energy and impact which can complicate the entire grief experience.

My childhood was tumultuous and my fractured family was only one aspect of the trauma I experienced. These emotional scars have imprinted my psyche. They continue to reveal untapped layers of grief fifty years my parents' divorce as I grieved the loss of my mom.

Why now? Why another layer of grief? Each time we endure a loss of any kind, other dimensions of grief can surface— sometimes connected to the present loss, but only indirectly. Under the broader grief umbrella, a more recent death opens sacred space for us to explore the losses endured throughout our entire lives. When my mom died, I reviewed my whole life with her. Surprisingly while grieving Mom, unresolved issues with my dad surfaced twenty-six years after his death. This prompted me to heal the next layers of grief connected to him.

Grief is the most complex, confusing, misunderstood, and often times ignored experience. There is much more within the journey than seeking to alleviate pain. Grief is illusive and resides within us until we intentionally embrace it.

As I furthered explored my emotions, I was shocked to discover buried anger related to my father. Here are the three significant revelations that came forward:

1. I hadn't fully known my dad. I only saw what he wanted me to see. I heard how others spoke of him: powerful and great. At nine, this was an age-appropriate perception and I held onto that image for many years. He had a lot of good qualities and was admired greatly in the community, but was unable to give me and our relationship the time and attention needed.
2. As I remembered my dad's wise words, "Don't quit. Do something every day toward your goals," a realization hit me like a

slap in the face. I thought, "Wait a minute, he quit. He left my mom, their marriage, and our family. I persevered for over thirty years in my own marriage even when times were tough." I took his advice—why didn't he?

3. Within my relationship mapping process, I revealed a childhood memory where we visited our newly-built, beautifully-designed homes. While in one part enjoying visiting the new construction with my dad, the structure felt energeticall y empty—like no one was home. Strikingly, it described our family's disconnection of that time to a T.

These realizations hit me hard. I felt deceived which led me into more healing work. Forgiveness was needed for my younger self who didn't know any different. I found myself needing to reconcile with the perceptions I established as a little girl to better understand the realities of adult relationship challenges.

Growing up and now being in a long-term marriage, I recognize each of us plays a part in our relationship's success or failure. In the unfolding of our grief journey, we often evaluate the roles roles, patterns, and dynamics we've held in our relationships throughout our lives.

After my parents divorced, my dad moved to another city. I didn't know it at the time, but I needed him—especially during my awkward adolescence. The trauma of their divorce, the broken emotional bonds, his absence, and the unaddressed grief within my family were devastating and beyond my comprehension. Although I felt special when Dad answered my calls, phoned me, and visited me once a week, I only realized later how connection with my dad on a daily basis could've helped me cope with life. Young girls need to feel treasured by their fathers to develop healthy self-esteem.

My dad did his best. I'm sure I told myself this common cliché to try to heal and stay in a relationship with my dad over the years. Adopting this belief helped me begin to take responsibility for finding help. However, telling myself that was his best caused me to negate and minimize my hurt and truth, never fully grieving these horrific losses.

My dad wasn't there a lot of the time, and I blamed myself, which created people-pleasing and approval-seeking tendencies.

It's important to note that I absolutely lived through a traumatic childhood with the family circumstanc es, but the results within my challenges and personality were also influenced by my ancestry and the cultural horrors of the Holocaust. All of which could've affected my belief systems, patterns, and self-esteem.

I disconnected from my authentic self, ignored my inner spirit, and searched for love and connection from others to validate my worth. Guess what? We can't find our worth in another person. Our worth is a divine quality. We are worthy simply because we exist. We are all children of God, have a right to live, and embody inherent value and worth.

Years ago, observing I discovered that I came from a "looking good" family. My family always acted sharp, dressed well, and appeared to have it together. We avoided showing the disheveled parts of ourselves on the outside. As the saying goes, we didn't air our dirty laundry in public. There were certain ways we were supposed to act and be. Raw emotions weren't acceptable because that would look messy and unattractive. This pattern wasn't simply about making my physical appearance more becoming, but appearing exceptional and virtuous, by performance or deed, in the hope of love and approval. I attempted to perfect my outer image to validate that my inner beauty and authentic self was enough.

My mom accessorized to the nines. She always made sure her make-up and hair were done perfectly, and then ensured we each dressed appropriately with our hair just right. If we were in a disagreement or fight, those big emotions had to be hidden. Sadly, I was told fairly often to 'put on a happy face' or "don't look so sour" which caused me to hide any disappointment or sadness. This pattern of hiding played out throughout my whole life—my authenticity and real emotions. Embodying moxie energy has served to empower me in grief and further stepping into higher self.

In Judaism, it's said that we have three images that we carry: the way we see ourselves, the way others see us, and the image we present to the world.

The most important image is further explained with the Jewish tenet of *B'tzelem Eloheim,* created in the image of God, carrying within our soul a spark our Creator. To love ourselves as God loves us, shining our light in the world, the world holds the potential to shift the entire consciousness of humanity.

Through my inner turmoil seeking to be something more, better, and different, I was actually pursuing a sense of belonging to feel enough and valued in the world. Only years later did I discover that I didn't have to be perfect. There's no crime in looking good. Bringing the best of ourselves into our relationships and our work is absolutely important. When we make ourselves look good, we feel good. Caring for ourselves raises our self-esteem and lifts our spirits. However, there might be an unconscious drive to improve our outward appearance that stems from underlying, unhealthy interpretations. Creating an image to fit in, measure up, or be valued hides our authentic selves and can often be an unconscious effort to validate our existence in the world.

My intention is to highlight two of my most challenging life patterns—shutting down and hiding. My grief simmered beneath the surface holding grudges and blaming others. While my dad was alive, I tried to heal the wounds of my childhood—the loss of my dad's presence.

When he became ill, we engaged in deep conversation which allowed me to be grateful that we'd connected before the end of his life. However, following Mom's death buried grief bubbled up to the surface revealing losses from long ago. Identifying their origin led me on a transformative path toward healing and taught me to embrace my difficult patterns as treasures.

American professor Joseph Campbell, author of *The Hero of a Thousand Faces,* identifies the self-development process of overcoming life's challenges known as the Hero's Journey. He states, "The cave you fear to enter holds the treasure you seek."Thus, our deepest challenges become our greatest treasures.

I've come to believe, deeply and profoundly, that my mom's nudging and excessive enthusiasm was her spirit encouraging me to overcome fear and doubt of discovering my true self. Through conversations during my mom's life and in our spirit-to-spirit dialogues, I learned that she didn't know these things yet and couldn't articulate the lessons of her experiences until she'd integrated the information fully. Within her spiritual consciousne ss, she now knows.

Navigating life's frustrations, I became aware of my limited coping skills. Realizing that I'd missed a whole segment of life's learning, I wondered, "Why hadn't Mom helped me understand life?" I suspect my mom was dealing her own pain and didn't know how to walk with me. I thought I was supposed to grow up and be an adult, yet didn't have the skills to navigate adulthood. This wasn't a temporary situation. As time went on, Mom became less and less emotionally available. I'm sure she was trying to survive the agony and uncertainty of starting a new life for herself, but she neglected some significant parenting responsibilities during this confusing and unpredictable period.

Even in my sixties, following my mom's death, I blamed myself for her withdrawal and lack of help after my parents' divorce.

My sisters told she tried to help me, but couldn't because of my anger, rebelliousness, and resistance to talking about my feelings. Of course, I didn't know my emotions at that time. Her emotional absence ripped through every part of my life. This is the surprising, unexpected exploration of suppressed loss that surfaces during the grief journey.

Although my mom possessed moxie throughout her life, after the divorce, she had to rediscover it. I resented my mom, held her accountable for the pain I experienced, and didn't understand why she couldn't be there for me emotionally. I thought something was wrong with me. These spiritual injuries impacted me at a cellular level and needed many years of deep inner work to heal my wounds—releasing resentment, self-forgiveness, and adopting new beliefs about myself, my family, and life.

Immersing in my grief, learning from the pain, and emerging from misunderstanding about myself into divine truths allowed me to embrace my own moxie. It took great effort to find my way from a down-trodden place—from blaming myself to knowing it wasn't my fault for my family's dissolution. Not knowing how to articulate what's happening and express feelings is not a wrong of a person, but a faulty system—patterns passed down through generations. Committing to grow through grief, being bold, standing tall with dignity and courage, and connecting with our values reveals our moxie. We build strength and resilience by continuing to face the challenges and truth within our family relationships.

I'm infinitely more aware today of the importance and power within the grief healing journey—-especially all the aspects of grief that crack open following a loss. In order to recognize the treasures within a relationship, we have to feel the impact of what worked and what didn't with our family members. By identifying the challenges experienced with my mom, I became a better mom. Now, with my own children, I build deeper connections by addressing my faults—past and present—hearing their requests of me and doing what's necessary to improve. Courageous conversations occur by showing up even when it's difficult and messy.

About twenty years ago, when I was studying Spiritual Psychology in my first master's program, we created a visual representati on of our family system called a *Genogram.* It illustrates family relationships, physical and mental health histories, as well as incidents and patterns within the family. While talking to my mom, a profoundly helpful memory popped into her head. When she was eighteen years old and her family was headed to New Orleans, a sudden change of plans occurred. My grandfather remained behind for business. My grandmother then had an extreme meltdown fearing that my grandfather was going to leave her. Mom was surprised and questioned my grannie. We discovered that my grannie's father left her mother at thirty years old with six children. As it turns out my great-grandfather was a womanizer. This story revealed why my mom feared abandonment for her entire life—questioning every time I had to leave her, wishing I could stay longer. This intergenerational trauma pattern was transmitted because the deep wounds, pains, hurts, and fears surrounding my great-grandfather's exit and the effect on the family were kept secret.

I'm certain Mom's awareness grew and she tried to transmit knowledge to me. However, I may not have been open or ready to receive her insights.

I'm struck by a lesson that continues to bless me even after her death. I saved some of my mom's voicemail messages—one of which was her wishing me a *"Happy Passover"* with her joyful Southern accent. It's somewhat inconsequential but profound. It was simply a gesture of love and caring to wish me and my family well for a holiday. The gift I received then and still to this day is her expression of heartfelt love—pure, genuine, and simple.

And yet, there were discrepancies. She didn't follow through in every aspect of our relationship. Still today, writing this, I am reconciling her inconsistencies. There were times she was present and also times when I experienced her absence. Teaching me to show up in one light is beautiful and yet brings pain from the occasions she wasn't there. Mom was an imperfect human being who had her own issues and difficulties which caused her pain and prevented her from physically showing up during different periods of her life.

My mom's wisdom, or maybe it's really divine wisdom that comes through my experience of her, was in how I received a simple seemingly insignificant phone message from her that taught me about consistently showing up. Throughout our lifespans, we do things because they're the "right'" thing to do, not even knowing where they came from, or what they're teaching us. Oddly, I thought I learned this way of being elsewhere and it seems strange to be an example I picked up from her. Caring actions like this nurture the spirit. It's about connection, being there for each other, and taking responsibility for the caring communication within the relationship. I didn't know the depth and profundity of her actions until the years following her death.

So many things that I reflected on after my mom's death revealed aspects of wisdom that I believe I couldn't possibly have faced while she was alive. I spent a lot of my life trying to heal the things I didn't think went well, the deep woundedness I experienced; and believing aspects of my life should've been different or easier. Having healed these wounds, I felt a great deal of freedom and ease with my mom in her last phase of life. However, after a death occurs every aspect of life with or without that person comes up for review. That's a significant part of the grief experience and what I believe leads us to a divine awakening and sends us on our transformative journey.

A well-known Zen proverb from Tibetan Buddhism, "When the student is ready, the teacher will appear," can offer hope, even the most stubborn like myself, will become ready when the right teacher appears. I've encountered many amazing teachers along my life's journey.

With every fiber of my being and the most vibrant desire to embody my greatest expression of moxie, I'm breaking the silence of pain and shame that has imprisoned me. Harboring shame is what causes us to hide and hold back our true essence. This task is not a simple one—certainly not a one-and-done journey—but rather a revelatory path of getting to know the truth of who we are. Creating perfected, outer images to look good played out unknowingly throughout much of my life. Over the years, I saw pieces of this looking-good pattern but didn't yet understand its origin or reason.

Over time, I've become aware of the many facets of these patterns and their underlying beliefs embedded in my psyche. However, even with my extensive inner work and employing alternative behaviors, I may have passed on inklings of these tendencies to my children. My mission has been to heal these parts within myself so I can live a healthier, more authentic life and break the cycles of inherited familial and cultural patterns for my children and the generations to come.

Our unresolved family patterns can show up in our grief. One morning after Mom died, I felt angry which surprised me because Mom and I had healed and resolved so much within our relationship. I was angry that Mom hadn't resolved our family's communication.

My sisters and I had gone our separate ways to deal with the powerful emotions of loss. I'd hoped for more connection with them during the earlier phases of grief. I wanted to be with my sisters, but realized we'd each need grieve in our own way.

I wished my mom had fixed the connections in our family before she died. Nothing was broken, but it felt like everything was broken. Sometimes, we don't know how to articulate what we're feeling, and often, there are just no words. None of us want to be left with unfinished business. We do our best to complete and heal all we can within our physical lives. Our loved ones pass the torch to us so that we can bring new light to our relationships, complete unfinished tasks, and further repair certain aspects of our world.

My sisters and I needed to recalibrate without Mom, individually and independently. Grief is a process that each person needs to do in their own unique way.

In my own personal grief recovery, I've discovered that intergenerational patterns are inherited simply by being a part of a family. Placing blame often happens when we want others to take responsibilit y for their actions. We assign fault when we're unconscious ly carrying the responsibility for the difficulties and trauma within our families. Each of us is responsible for the individual parts we play in our relationships.

Healing these internal wounds clears the way for new perspective and better communication. As we recognize the intergenerational patterns within our families, we can address them and affect change.

According to shame and vulnerability researcher and professor Brené Brown, blame is the discharging of anger, discomfort, and pain. Blame gets activated when we we're not acknowledging our owninner experience. Anger in grief comes from an extreme sense of powerlessness over our emotions and situations, the change and disruption in our relationships, and a basic fear of the unknown.

We inherit intergenerational patterns as we live and experience each year of life. Internalized energy from our unhealed trauma simmers under the surface and when unresolved, is carried forward into the next generation.

As mentioned earlier, my dad's family escaped Germany in 1939 just after Kristallnacht, referred to as the Night of Broken Glass, when the Nazis turned against the Jews—our people, homes, synagogue, and livelihood.

Dad carried this trauma with him and would've benefited greatly from therapy.

It's my understanding that Dad didn't believe in therapy for himself. Perhaps this was because of the stigma attached to seeking mental health support at that time. As a result, he didn't share (at least not with me) the impact of his experience in Nazi Germany—his family's escape, ethnic persecution, loss of their home, safety, and way of life. I've often wondered how these events might have also affected his faith and trust in the world.

I suspect that Dad silently carrying this trauma resulted in limiting beliefs I later identified within myself: not being enough and not wanting to make waves or be seen. This is an example of inherited intergenerational, cultural patterns that can unconsciously influence us throughout our lives.

Dad never spoke about the devastating trauma toward his family—the relentless threats, blame, and shame nor the effect of being forced from their home or migrating tothe United States. He didn't share any of the trials for challenges of being a Jew in the world and I only learned about these difficulties from my sisters.

Ignoring our traumas can temporarily bury them but does not erase them. We cannot shut ourselves off from the effects. We can periodically distract ourselves until our buttons get pushed and unexpected, disruptive behaviors surface the trauma still remains within us. Acknowledging the wounds mean it really happened. As a child, I wasn't aware of his childhood experiences or his thought processes. The energy of my dad's difficulties trusting authority, humanity, and the systems of the world were unconscious ly passed onto me and my sisters. His unexpressed stored emotions seeped out and ripped through our family.

Learning my family and cultural history of persecution, pillage, and turmoil, I can imagine and feel terror, uncertainty and an internal need to hide that I believe carried forward.

Despite our best efforts to suppress, move beyond, or change our past, cultural, family and relational trauma is transferred onto future generations. Many silently store their grief out of fear. It is difficult to articulate and unravel the compounde d layers of ancestral loss and trauma. These are often the wounds that are activated during the following the death of loved one opening a pathway for healing. Courageously giving voice to our pain within the tapestry of our lives is how we break these inherited patterns.

Processing flashes of memories and connections to historical times within my family and within our ethnic lineage, I've discovered resonant experiences that no one could verify. My emotions and the energetic sensations tell me the truth of my soul experience. Like my family, I, too have felt my Jewish identity and livelihood threatened where the feelings of anxiety and urge to hide were undeniable. These invaluable insights have helped me piece together the puzzle of the emotional trauma of my family's journey.

When my dad died, I realized how little I knew about our family history. I hadn't been interested and needed to focus on my inner healing the first twenty years of my adult life.

I didn't try to connect with him spiritually after he died. Honestly, it took me a long time to process my abandonment resulting from my parents' divorce. Intellectually, I knew Dad left Mom, but I felt the family bonds dissolving and was missing crucial connection during my formative years.

In 2019, recovering from two car accidents and experiencing tremendous anxiety and upheaval, my sister Cathy shared about our dad's possible challenges with anxiety—worrying about money, always checking our doors, and treasuring all his books. Interestingly, I do the same. All my books are sacred and rarely give any away. Cathy explained that Dad had witnessed the German soldiers burning all the Jewish books within their community. Hearing this history helped me understand my familial quirks about connecting with money, ensuring the safety of my home, and holding onto almost all my books.

During the grief journey, it is surprising, and sometimes shocking, to witness the different layers of awareness that arise further teaching us about our internal makeup. These stories validate my intuitive connections to my Jewish ancestry. Within my meditations and by following the internal energetic experience, I receive inner messages the reveal remnants of the Holocaust and the deep physical sensations of what they may have endured.

These internal processes allowed me to feel the dehumanization of Jews in that time. The Jewish people were devalued and kept alive only for other's pleasure and satisfaction. It's reasonable to understand how we could be significantly affected by such horrific turmoil—even generations later. As energetic beings (which we all are), our souls and bodies are imprinted with experiences. We can feel similar sensations as our family members who came before us. This begins to explain how the soul's essence continues with the memories of our loved ones. This is one way we experience intergenerational, inherited family patterns, which can be both traumatic and beautifully powerful.

Within my consciousness, I've had visual images and sensations showing me the Nazis laughing as they took from the Jews. Stored within was debris from past generations that we'd never be enough, always have to strive to be better or more, and that we wouldn't have a rightful place in the world. Many other cultures experience this annihilation, dehumanization, exclusion, and racism which resides within the body and mind inhibiting a full life. This inner intelligence that is eternally connected to my ancestors guides me to learn from my family heritage and lineage to heal the past and clear the path for future generations.

Energetically, I'm often visited by deceased spirits — patients, family members, in cemeteries, and during the time of of the Holocaust. I feel their spiritual essence and presence, and often have spiritual conversations with them.

As spiritual beings, our souls can travel to different places in time and different realms of consciousness as well as varying ages within our lifespan. During these deep processes where my soul travels through time, powerful dialogues and physiological sensations shine a light on how Jews might have suffered and then offers me guidance for elevating awareness and healing the world. Acknowledging the effects of these impressions within my body has helped me to understand myself and some of my deepest fears awakening me to the greater truth within my soul—my addictions, control, disconnection, insecurities, and the effects of my trauma history. This led me to recognize and nourish my gifts and strengths that developed such as my compassion, gratitude, loving, passion, perseverance, understanding, and wisdom which allows me to guide others.

Years ago, no one knew how to talk about energetic spiritual connections. We know much more now. Embracing these parts and experiences answered many of my life's existential questions about meaning, purpose, and value. There is a place inside each of us that knows our own experience which calls on us to seek to understand ourselves better at each juncture of life.

Honoring all humanity is still a challenge in our daily lives, workplaces, and communities. Bringing awareness to these difficulties provides us opportunities for healing by deepening our connection to the places inside where we carry buried ancestral wounds.

Several years ago, at a previous job where a series of difficulties occurred, I associated my feelings with what I sensed my dad might've experienced as a Jew being unfairly and unreasonably attacked earlier in his life in Germany. As a chaplain, I'm a mandated reporter and required to report when I suspect potential abuse. In the course of my early hospice work, some of my patients' stories raised suspicion of potential elder abuse and warranted reporting to the appropriate protective agencies. My employer at that time minimized the seriousness of the implications, brushed it off as patient peculiarities, and dismissed the need for further investigation. My concerns were disregarded. I felt attacked retaliated against me for advocating for my patients' safety.

While processing these difficult patient scenarios in meditation one day, a sensation of spiritual energy arose with anxiety and fear, and I felt as though someone was shooting at me. Then an image surfaced where I saw a young boy and had an impression that this child was my father while still in Germany. This picture revealed him dashing from buildings and ducking behind them to protect himself. I had the sense that the Germans were shooting at him. My father's experiences, combined with my rising sensations and images that were undeniably powerful, profoundly connected me to my feelings and produced a sense that I was also being attacked similarly to gunfire in my work situations. Interestingly, no one in my family seemed to know for certain if this happened to my dad. However, I do know that later in life he was attacked for taking non-discriminatory, unbiased actions on behalf of the African American community. The association was very real, offering me a framework for similar feelings and sensations and a way to comprehend what was happening through a spiritual lens, providing further learning for my soul.

From what I've learned about my dad's experiences I can only imagine the impact of the cultural trauma he must have endured. I wholeheartedly believe that he consciously chose not to verbalize the degradation and dehumanization I presume he experienced. Rather, he compartmentalized and internalized it. This was how he survived and thrived, but I suspect he stored it in his body which later may have contributed to the development of his ALS (Amyotrophic lateral sclerosis is a nervous system disease that affects nerve cells in the brain and spinal cord.

ALS is often called Lou Gehrig's disease after the baseball player who was diagnosed with it). I believe he buried his trauma which significantly affected his body and shortened his life.

I've concluded that he needed to charge forward, rise above, and make a place for himself in the free world—for himself and later for us. I recognize today that facing this unresolved trauma head-on might've devastated and destroyed him, and therefore, made it impossible to create and pave the way for our family to live fruitful lives.

One of my spiritual practices for processing inner experiences is to engage in spirit-to-spirit conversations with loved ones. Here is a profound communication with my deceased father taken from my journal writings:

> *Candi*: Hi Dad—Today I'm writing about the intergenerational patterns that I've perceived from the family, from you, and others. I feel these exchanges in my body, weird to many but yet very real to me. I look at and process all that still plagues me with body image and weight. I process deeply to connect the dots and release the judgments. This morning, I released a belief about denying myself love based on my appearance which feels very real and powerful and connected to your German experience. You never talked about anything like this, and I wasn't aware of it when you were alive. You died so early so I wasn't able to ask you. What can you tell me now from your spirit essence? I don't want to presume, and yet I need to tell the truth of my experience.
>
> *Dad*: Hello Doll, I'm so glad you're writing to me now. You know I wasn't spiritually connected during my living years. Now, I see things for what they are. I held everything inside because I didn't know how to talk about it. We just had to hold it in to survive. I didn't understand that it would be

healing to talk about it. I felt trapped a lot in my body, which may have contributed to my ALS.

Your sense and awareness are accurate, Candi. It was horrific. We were who we were—Jews—and were attacked for our identity. This wasn't new, but as it escalated, the destruction was out of control. At eleven years old, when we left Germany, I already felt powerless and defeated. To bury it was the only way to survive and discover a safer life. I see now that it stayed with me. I don't know if I could've even begun to unpack the terror I felt.

It makes perfect sense to me now that these experiences are transmitted energetically. Courageously unpacking these messages so that you heal opens the space and possibilities for others to heal and be free. I know that this is not easy for you. You feel it all in your body, and at times, it physically hurts. Take care of yourself. I also know your belief that you are a channel for healing. Allowing this awareness and powerful vibrations to energetically come through releases and brings relief for you.

I love you, Doll—Dad.

Candi: Thank you, Dad. My heart, jaw, ears, and teeth hurt. What is that? Do you know?

Dad: Yes, it's the pain of having a voice. Bring it for the highest good—for hope and healing. This is who you are.

This conversation with my dad was twenty-six years after his death. As I still unpack layers of grief, I know my process is purposeful for writing this book. This dialogue gave me great comfort, further healing, and more courage to speak out. I trust these spirit-to-spirit conversations often far more than I would speaking to a live person. This spiritual consciousness brings forward the truth from my heart and soul. My worries were dissolved and transformed. Deeply connecting with my body's physical sensations and precious emotions guides me to my divine truth.

Chapter 8

SPIRITUAL GROWTH IN LIFE AND DEATH

*"The pain of grief awakens our heart, nudges our spirit,
expands our soul awareness, and connects us with
a sacred energy that lies beyond the human experience."*

—Chaplain Candi Wuhrman

Heart and soul connections are genuine, powerful, and transformative, and ground us in our sacred light. Navigating highly charged emotions, embracing grief and loss, forgiving judgments, releasing limiting beliefs, and reframing misalignments provide avenues for transforming challenging relationships—even from the grave.

To further clarify and illustrate how intergenerational patterns manifest, I want to share a time when my sense of belonging felt threatened, seemingly related to my historical-cultural trauma. The following incidents after Mom's death illuminated how loss can and trigger deeper uncertainties and vulnerabilities within our psyche that needs to be reconciled.

Just over a year after Mom died, one morning while getting ready for work, I experienced a tachycardia event (a very rapid heartbeat), which left me extremely shaky for hours. Uncertain of the cause and still out of balance, one of our hospice doctors strongly recommended that I go to urgent care to be checked out. While in the clinic, my cognition became impaired. With an alter mental state, I was sent to the hospital for a higher level of care and more extensive evaluation.

Hours later, the doctors determined that no catastrophic event had occurred—such as a stroke, heart attack, or brain bleed—instructed to wear a heart monitor for two weeks. At my follow-up appointment, my physician reluctantly diagnosed the episode as a panic attack and recommended I take time off from work. Just hearing her suggestion, my chest tightened. I interpreted my doctor's recommend ation to mean that must be inadequately managing my stress and that implication was too much to bear.

Along life's journey, if God and the Universe need your attention, incidents will continue until you wake up. First, it's a pebble, then a rock, and if we don't pay attention, it becomes a boulder. After the cardiac event, I had a knee injury and feared I'd torn my ACL (anterior cruciate ligament) again, but thankfully, I didn't. Then the "alarm clock" got a bit louder, and I had two car accidents just three weeks apart while out seeing my hospice patients. I injured my back but ignored the pain, which only got worse.

Then our son, Josh, had a traumatic rock-climbing accident, which ultimately got my attention. I finally woke up. God was tapping me on the shoulder, and several other parts of my body, asking me to pay attention—right here, right now. Until this event, I hadn't paused to listen to the message being presented to me. I was just pushing forward, thinking I was in charge.

After considerable time on medical leave, I recognized the physical, emotional, mental, and spiritual effects of all of this trauma. I felt extremely vulnerable, which triggered historical trauma. The chaos from the series of events involving the worker's compensation process, reliving the auto accidents through extensive medical appointments, the financial burden, and the disconnection from my hospice team reactivated remnants of previous trauma. These experiences produced a vast amount of grief that involved a multitude of losses—mobility, livelihood, connection, trust, and safety—resulting in deep isolation and causing me to question my value.

Something else beneath the surface was triggered. I realized I'd resisted taking time off after the tachycardia episode because I was unconsciously still trying to prove my worth and value as a newer member of the team. Interestingly, related to my inherited cultural and family trauma, deep connections had been lost. I feared I would no longer belong in my hospice family.

Resurfacing trauma and fear can often present barriers to seeing our truth in the moment. In reality, I already knew my team valued me, but this is how the effects of past trauma can bubble up during tumultuous times. After processing yet more layers of grief and the related emotions, my perspective was clear again.

Organizational situations can resemble an individual's family system, which awakens us to the issues within ourselves that need healing. My company's actions and responses following my car accidents and during my recovery disconnected, inconsistent, incongruent, and unaccommodating. Their words said they cared, but their actions didn't align. This strangely mimicked my family's somewhat inconsistent ways which triggered extreme imbalance and uncertainty. Mistrust and a sense of unreliability surfaced when I realized my company wouldn't take care of me after these accidents which resembled the loss of trust I experienced in my childhood. It takes great moxie to face the uncertaintie s and inner turmoil that is stirred by life's unexpected events presents opportunities to heal.

I understood my job couldn't accommodate the health needs of after my back injury, and another position within the company was not available. I became aware that God was showing me a different path. I resigned and began a private chaplaincy, coaching, and counseling practice.

In my new business, I feared being more visible. This was *not* about looking good, but more about being real, vulnerable, and transparent while offering value. Facing these changes, I continued grieving my mom and wished she could share with me how she showed up despite her fear. She would've said, "Get going. Take those first steps. That's how you act boldly and move forward courageously."

As a mom with my two children, I always thought I'd learned better ways of parenting and certainly wouldn't make the same mistakes as my parents. I have acted differently in a lot of ways. However, I inadvertently adopted patterns I disliked, only I did them in other ways. At times, I created confusion when I wanted to foster harmony. Children learn from what they see, not what we say.

After my parents' divorce and my mom became a therapist, she was constantly trying to figure me out by asking probing questions. I often felt as though she treated me as one of her clients. I then became a chaplain who also counsels and consequently asked my children a multitude of questions, which gave them a similar type of feeling. I only later realized that my mom did it to help me, but it felt like she wanted to fix me when I wasn't broken. I was just growing and learning. I asked my kids questions to stay connected and abreast of their activities. My mom and I produced the same confusion from the energy of fear because of unresolved family issues. When life's events cause inner disturbance and uncertainty within relationships, may project our own unsettled energy into our conversations giving an untended message.

Two years before Mom died, our daughter, Michelle, began dating the man who is now her husband, Alex. He is quite a bit older than she is, so initially, I was concerned. However, I realized that imposing my beliefs and expectations on my children was unacceptable. Michelle has always been free to choose what's right for her. Michelle was thoughtfully choosing her life path.

One afternoon I shared this with my mom. She listened intently and then said, "Candi, you just need to love her. I wish I'd loved you more when you brought boys home."

I was touched by her words and recognized that my mom was reconciling with all the times she had disapproved of and doubted my choices. I was in awe and deeply felt this energetic healing within my heart. I decided to accept Mom's guidance and just love my daughter through all her choices and experiences.

Based on my upbringing, I believed that a person seeks a partner close to their own age. I assumed, incorrectly, that Michelle would follow my beliefs. My short-sightedness pushed me and called on me to seek a deeper truth, honoring my daughter's choice of a partner who aligns with her soul. We all have a divine right to make different choices.

Michelle's decision to choose the right person for her broke the cycles of cultural and familial patterns. She had every right to seek the soulmate perfect for her. My feelings were about my inability to see beyond my conditioning. The experience called on me to reassess my beliefs and values about love and marriage. I knew two things: I wanted Michelle to be true to herself, and I wanted to maintain my connection with her.

I took Mom's divine guidance to heart and began to feel my daughter's love for Alex. I honor and trust their soul connection. On our first visit to their home, Alex said with a big hug, "Don't worry. I will take care of Michelle." And I know they love each other deeply.

I spent years trying to conform to my parents' unspoken expectations rather than being true to myself. Healing these wounds allowed me to trust that my children would be guided by their inner spirits.

When our children choose a different path than we've expected, we have to look at what's difficult for us. We need to examine the origin of our own conditioning, expectations, and patterns and recognize the demands we've placed on ourselves instead. This means it's about us, not them. Doing my inner work released my fear and expectations—energetically freeing Michelle to follow her heart more easily, feeling my love, connection, and openness.

My words cannot fully express the profound benefit of embracing these miracles of transformation. I knew Michelle would always go forward with her heart's desires. Releasing my expectations of a particular outcome made Michelle's journey easier. My mom's miraculous acknowledgment of her shortcomings cleared the way for a more accepting, expansive, and loving experience all the way around.

In her book, *The Resilient Spirit,* author Polly Young-Eisendrath discusses the transformation of suffering into insight and renewal. She notes that although transforming overwhelming childhood adversity is quite challenging, we can gain strength and learn resilience by walking through the lingering pain of the experience. Taking responsibility for our part in our pain and seeking a larger context of meaning can empower us with greater self-determination and even self-confidence. I would also add that navigating through challenges and realizing that we can overcome them deepens our faith.

I believe difficult conditions endured in childhood can be resolved and changed through our awareness of our situation and our development. Anyone who overcomes childhood adversity, turns their life around, and works to improve the world has much to teach us all. This is the essence of healing our patterns for a blessing and the epitome of embodying the quality of moxie.

As mentioned earlier, some relationships cannot be addressed until our loved one dies. At times, discussing family issues may not feel safe, and we may need to defend the ideal image of our family to stay involved. Unraveling such relationships or personalities may be too troubling until the person has passed.

I mostly speak of my mom and dad's deaths, my grief-healing processes, and my learning and transformations through both my personal losses and professional insights as a hospice chaplain. The notion that certain circumstances cannot be processed until a person has moved on applies to additional types of losses as well. The pain within grief is often connected to many components of the relationship and needs to be addressed as it arises.

During the grief journey, waves of confusion reveal emotionally charged unfinished business. These realizations often need deeper exploration to heal their broken bonds. The Grief Recovery Institute teaches that when we experience loss, we invariably have undelivered emotional expressions which can leave relationships incomplete, further burdening an already painful situation.

Physical losses, such as:

- death
- divorce
- parents' divorce
- family addiction
- financial devastation
- any type of abuse, illness, or trauma

are equally as damaging as intangible losses, such as the absence of:

- comfort
- connection
- faith
- safety
- stability
- trust

We often cannot deliver these messages during someone's lifetime due to various reasons such as age, the nature of the relationship, or particular circumstances. This unfinished business emotionally binds us to the experience of loss. The pain blocks us from learning from our life experiences and hinders our ability to fully appreciate the time we spent with our loved one. When we deliver these painfully ladened messages, we clear the residue on our hearts and are then able to recognize the spiritual essence of life and death along with the wholeness of our loved one's soul as well as our own.

Hindsight always presents a clearer vision and can become our best teacher. Sometimes we may not even realize the impact of a relationship, including our feelings, the messages we have internalized, and the meaning it has brought to our lives, until we experience the depth of our grief.

Healing the issues of the heart within our relationships is an ongoing process that can offer us our greatest spiritual growth. After our loved one has passed, our environment may feel safer, enabling us to confront our relationship challenges. We can then explore new insights and recalibrate our lives without our loved ones, which allows us to come into our own.

In the last few years of Mom's life, while I was preparing for a virtual job interview, she reminded me to smile, emphasizing the importance of looking good on the outside—for the camera, for the show. It felt like she was saying, "Be pretty, don't be real, just look good." But there are times when a smile does not match the situation and would not be the most authentic expression. When we think of distressing situations, we don't smile.

Mom's instructions could have been misinterpreted as "Don't think; Your looks are more important than your brains." This is a common message for many women. Engaging authentically incorporates multiple facial expressions. Intellectually, Mom knew this, but her emotional wounds caused her to want us, and herself, to be put together so that the image looked just right—an arbitrary "right" look.

Some children may be unaffected by these types of comments. However, I decided a long time ago to pay attention to my feelings, look deeper inside for the truth, and learn from my challenges to become the best person I could be. These illogical remarks were initiated by her fear of not looking good enough, and she unconsciously projected her discomfort onto me. I then took on this insecurity as my own—yet another example of an inherited familial pattern.

Psychological pioneer Carl Jung said projections are anything that lay in the unconscious part of one's personality. These projections arise unconsciously and unintentionally. Inherited familial patterns are the unhealed wounds that we project onto others—often our children. Fortunately, or unfortunately, that makes us human. We parent in the way we were parented until we find our practices ineffective, sometimes even harmful. Then we learn a better way.

Minimizing the impact of our parenting mistakes, brushing off disruptive events, and adopting the falsely held belief that kids are resilient is carelessly inappropriate and, in my strong moxie-like opinion, negligent.

The saying "kids are resilient" is often an assertion thrown at a kid's discomfort to give parents a false sense of hope that the child's turmoil will blow over. The truth is kids don't just get over "it." It stays with us. Kids may hear such a statement and fear that they're wrong for having feelings relating to a traumatic event—large, small, or seemingly insignificant.

We often don't know that we've made a mistake until the aftereffects are revealed. If our inner child's spirit was minimized, squelched, or in any way marginalized, we can explore our childhood difficulties at any particular age. As adults, we can then recognize similar patterns occurring for our children and end the cycle of harm for the next generation.

Humbly and vulnerably asking for help, allows us to embrace the wealth of available resources: new tools, practices, and healing modalities.

My mom was beautiful, always looked good, and took pride in her appearance. However, she didn't always think she looked good. Mom always had her makeup on, her hair styled, wore fashionable clothing with precious rings, necklaces, and earrings (even though they hurt her unpierced earlobes), and of course, always wore her red lipstick. Mom wore shiny costume watches and bracelets matching every outfit. I adopted this same pattern and inherited these color-coordinated accessories. Interestingly, costume jewelry could be a appropriate metaphor for the masks we wear.

From the time I was a teenager, I remember my mom pausing in front of the bathroom mirror before going out and asking, "Look okay?" This private intimate moment always left me with confusion and further questioning: "Why was she asking me? and Was no one else to know that Mom was uncertain about her appearance? Just holding the secret was burden enough.

Was this a result of my parents' divorce? I suspect this pattern is connected to multiple cultures and societal thinking common to women. I'm guessing that similar multi-generational core patterns existed in my maternal lineage. I wasn't exposed directly. However, I know what I saw, heard, and felt. I loved my mom just the way she was, but I saw her questioning herself.

Concerned about writing such material about my mom and breaking a secret, I engaged in this spirit-to-spirit written dialogue:

> *Candi*: Mom, is this okay to bring forward? I feel scared to be honest about what I saw, heard, and felt. I wouldn't want to defame you. I'm afraid of what others will think, feel, or fear by my sharing this awareness and these conclusions that have brought me clarity, made me better, and more aware in my life.
>
> *Mom*: Yes, Candi, it is more than okay. It is necessary, and I'm calling on you, your courage and moxie, to bring it forward for the healing for all who will take it in. This is true. I wasn't aware of these things, or why I was doing them. It's not bad or good. Bringing awareness to these idiosyncrasies is not to produce shame but to clear and release it so each of us can have a freer inner life and show up in the fullness of who we are—who we're meant to be. Go to it.

Little internal spiritual conversations such as this with my mom helped me to move forward. These intermittent connections inspired me to keep on going. Although, looking back, still afraid, I had hit a turning point. Do I turn back out of fear, or do I consciously choose to trust the spiritual guidance propelling me to forge ahead courageously on this path?

With that said, as I struggled to reveal these inadequacies, once again, I wrestled with my vulnerabilities—being seen, telling my truth, and exposing myself to the opinions of and possible dislike of others.

Internally, I asked, "Why now, Mom? Why write this stuff now? Why divulge what I've struggled with so much in my life? I feel it all when I bring it up, and I feel guilty for implying that I got it from you, Dad, and our family."

I heard my mom answer in my head, "Now is the time. It is not defaming me, criticizing me, or blaming me for your discomfort. This is about speaking out about what so many of us, particularly women, have struggled with for eons—trying to be more—when we are already enough. I didn't know, and now I do. We don't have to wait until we leave this earth to know these things. Bringing this truth forward is how you will make my memory a blessing."

Mom continued, "You remember, I worked with women for years on self-esteem and assertiveness training. I suppose I was trying to learn it for myself at the same time. This is why our lives look confusing as we age. We are not the same people because we continue to grow and change. Who I was when you were a young child is not the same person I became when you were a teenager. Sadly, I didn't know how those changes would affect you and couldn't have been aware of them as potential problems for you."

We learn as we grow, but the integration of the lessons takes time.

This is also why it's important to bring these issues to the forefront now. Sometimes our children see us when we are better people having learned a few lessons, but earlier experiences in their formative years impact them. Even though we as parents have changed in some areas, to ignore our past challenges is to minimize and negate our children's similar emotions and can inhibit our connection with them.

There have been occasions where my perfectionism has set the ball rolling. I wanted certain things to look effortlessly pristine, from the towels folded perfectly in the linen closet to feeling the urge to correct something—anything. I now process and heal the underlying causes of my perfectionistic behaviors when they arise. When something feels off, out of order, or uncertain, my angst stirs my need to control. This was also a family pattern.

Very early one morning while our son Josh was staying with us, he was preparing for a camping trip. I noticed he left a sticker on his new cooler. In my infamous helping mode, I offered to easily remove it for him. I thought peeling off the sticker would leave a clean, sleek, and perfect look. This was part of my own need to fix things.

Josh permitted me to remove the sticker as long as it didn't leave a mess. Happily, I jumped right in. I had a task—something to do for him. I was needed. I couldn't get the thing off, made a bigger mess, and was unable to remove the sticky residue.

Did you know that if you don't remove stickers before their first washing, they don't come off easily? Who knew?

Josh got frustrated with my slow progress, grabbed the steel wool, and quickly scrubbed the ice chest, scratching the plastic. My attempt to ease my unidentified angst, and my son's reaction to the situation before sunrise, completely annoyed my husband, Arnie. He was still trying to sleep and offered to simply purchase a new cooler.

Unknowingly, these efforts toward perfection can be subtly running within our psyche. Admittedly, I set the ball rolling on this one. Then, in short order, all of us wanted the cooler to look good, and in Arnie's case, he wanted Josh to feel more comfortable and to go back to sleep.

Josh later gave us a couple of his small appliances as he prepared for a move. With new insight, I glanced at those stickers that he left and smiled with acceptance, reminded of our imperfections and the uniqueness we possess. I realized that appliance stickers can alert us to potential dangers with their use. In addition, the stickiness of a situation can be the catalyst for further healing (not to mention a whole lot of humor).

Seeking to look good is about our appearance and also about wanting to portray a particular image to the world. Wanting to feel desired and valued is the energy fueling the image we present in our lives, our families, our relationships, and our vocations.

Striving to prove our worth and value is a soul sickness of epic proportions and far more debilitating than the coronavirus pandemic. Our unacknowledged sense of unworthiness and lack of self-love are squelching our inner spirits.

Up until now, our society has skirted around these spiritual injuries only placing a band-aid over the wounds, but not fully healing the inner turmoil. We are valuable simply because we exist and have many opportunities to heal. Learning these spiritual lessons, who we are as divine spirits, is a lifelong journey.

Throughout my writing, I frequently asked for inspiration and intuition, particularly around challenging topics, which gave me the courage to take my next steps. When I stepped into this venture, I had no idea the magnitude of the transformational journey ahead. At perfect times, experiences just magically happened, teaching me the very lesson needed to illustrate how intergenerational patterns and cultural karma transmit to subsequent generations. This is one of the mystical ways spiritual evolution occurs leading us on a path of awakening, growth, and change.

Striving to look good with a desire to portray a particular image that is driven by fears of not being enough is a core insecurity energetically transmitted down the family line. I believe my mom picked up fearful energy from her mom (whose father also left the family when she was young). That unspoken insecure, uncertain energy carried through life situations. Then I unknowingly absorbed it and believed it was mine.

Energetic transmission occurs merely by exposure to a person. More specifically, when someone is carrying unacknowle dged charged emotions such as anger, fear, and shame. This has been especially revealed with babies in utero and with young children absorbing their mother's emotions, and then carrying those feelings into their lives.

The personality trait of perfectionism results from our fear and anxiety. Although Mom denied that she was a perfectionist, and it could've lessened throughout her years, it showed up regularly as she prepared our home for guests—specifically on holidays and special occasions.

Mom wanted everything to be perfect, and I followed suit. A properly set table, glistening silver, and tidy cupboards and closets presented an all-together image to family and friends. In my case, I attempted to hide my own organic, imperfect human nature.

I may have inadvertently passed these patterns on to my children. If so, hopefully, the energy will lessen each time I address it within my own consciousness. Those sticky remnants on Josh's plastic cooler were not life-altering. That singular situation with my son was not traumatic. However, the angst that urged me to want to control was a shortcoming within my personality and spirit that needed attention. These weak spots have been my hurdles to overcome, so that I could engage with myself more comfortably in my own skin and break the pattern of passing it on to future generations.

Over the last thirty-five years, as these issues became clearer, I could address them in a healthier way. Each time we own these quirky behaviors, we shine light upon them, bring more balance, and transform them into valuable energy. Perfectionism can shift from an obsession to meet an inordinate standard to useful attention to detail.

Before beginning my healing journey, having issues equated to brokenness, inadequacy, and insufficiency that needed to be fixed. Confusion and pain related to my trauma led me to seek healing and spiritual transformation. A soul-centered life is found as we acknowledge the issues that have troubled our spirit and hindered our ability to wholeheartedly engage in the world.

Both the beauty and the beast within us reveal those messy parts we want to hide or think we should. Being vulnerable by sharing our insecurities builds connection within relationship and helps us recognize our commonalities with all humanity. Ironically, sharing the truth of who we are sets us free to live more vibrantly. Stepping into our moxie means releasing the parts and patterns of ourselves that no longer serve us, connecting with the great divine spirit that resides within us, and learning to express ourselves more fully.

The greatest blessing that comes from healing family trauma messaging is a new perspective. Years of pain, irritation, and hurt released shifting my consciousness and fostering new awareness, connection, and insight.

The biggest blessing that comes after healing the inner stickiness of family circumstances is seeing a new perspective.

Through my teens and into my adult years, I felt an internal stickiness with my mom—an indescribable enmeshment. I never really knew what it was or how to describe it. I believe it was her over-caring trying to replace what I lost after my parents' divorce.

While studying Spiritual Psychology in graduate school, I began feeling an overbearing sense that my mom was in charge of my life, but at the time didn't understand what was happening energetically. As stayed with the uncomfortable sensations and processed it more deeply. I questioned: *Was she my life force?*

Traveling the energetic sensations within my body and spirit brought my awareness to a series of memories. Listening deeply to the guidance of my inner voice led me to connect to profound interpretations.

My mom told me over and over with such pride and empowerment that she was responsible for the miracle of my life. She explained to me many times that she'd had a miscarriage before I came me. She proudly said the doctor told her not to get pregnant, but she did anyway. I interpreted her energy and words to mean that she was the reason I existed.

As a kid, I wondered why she was telling me this. Later, I wondered if she went against medical advice, thought she knew better, and might have been putting both of us in danger with the pregnancy. I felt angry and confused.

Within my deep inner process, I sensed an image of an umbilical cord and felt this emotional hold on me literally at my navel. My perception was that I energetically bought into the idea that my mom was my emotional lifeline, although I later saw it in a new light.

By this time, my relationship with God had been evolving for fifteen years, and I knew God as the Creator of my life. Ultimately, this profound awakening allowed me to make complete sense of my past emotions. Cutting the emotional umbilical cord with my mom was needed and ultimately freed me.

By processing the layers of confusion and grief, energetically releasing these unhealthy misunderstandings, I realigned with my true Source and put Mom in a proper perspective. I then received an awareness that my mom never intended anything disempowering or malicious.

Within my regular meditation process, I energetically released these unhealthy misunderstandings, realigned with my true Source, and put my mom in a proper perspective. After processing the layers of confusion and grief, I am aware that my mom never intended anything disempowering or malicious.

Later, Mom shared that she had a strong sense that I was destined to be in this world and my life force she felt driving her decision and excitement to share this with me. This felt more authentic and empowering.

Years ago, Mom presented a community talk to women entitled "The Golden Years." My sister Cathy sent me Mom's handwritten notecards for her presentation describing Mom's message as "magic and miracles."

Reading Mom's notes made me realize how little I knew of her beliefs about life and her views on how to live fully. Mom had a faith in humanity that far surpassed anything I'd ever seen. She was regularly teased for being gullible and shocked when bad things happened.

Now I see her trusting zeal for life as her superpower. I only interpreted her enthusiastic optimism as an attempt to push me in the direction of her desires. Mom's understanding of life was much deeper than I gave her credit for, and I wish she could have transmitted more of that to me earlier in my life.

The two caveats preventing that transmission were the rate at which she understood life and my receptivity—the timing of my maturity and my willingness to learn from her.

Another limitation could also be true. If she attempted to share her learning, it may not have been the soul lesson that was appropriate for me. We each have our particular soul lessons to learn in our lifetime.

In Mom's scribbled notes, she showed me her vulnerability, humility, faith, and trust. Transparently, she shared that she was at a complete loss for the words to begin this talk as the date approached.

Courageously, she admitted to her audience that twelve years earlier, before her speaking on effective parenting, I'd run away from home—at 16 years old. She was challenged as a parent and living the messiness of motherhood. My mom shared authentically that she was tested by my rebellion and equally challenged by the effects of aging during *her* golden years. Although there were no specific dates noted for this presentation, the speaking invitation was timely when Mom needed to draw on her moxie. Based on the ages mentioned, I figured it was within the first few months after my stepfather, Jeff, had died. She was pretty torn up by Jeff's absence and needed tremendous strength and courage to go forward.

Mom acknowledged in her notes that many of us bought into a myth that once we've struggled in our earlier years, the next phase of our lives should be without its challenges—smooth and untroubled. She writes, "It is not like that for most of us. Life is full of challenges."

Mom spoke brilliantly, boldly, and soberly about our vulnerable aging bodies, our anticipated loss of loved ones, our mortality, and our need for coping skills when these life events occur. Just as my sister characterized the talk as "magic and miracles," Mom suspected that her audience was expecting magic solutions for the perfect golden years. With pure unadulterated moxie, she said, "The magic pill is the magic we can create within ourselves."

I was stunned to read this profoundly forward-thinking, radically bold idea that we have the power within us to create magic (from my mom!).

Mom emphatically asked the rhetorical questions: "Can we cope with aging?" and "How can we prepare now?" and then she stated, "I believe we can, and we should."

Of course, these are notes from her speech, so I'm not exactly clear about her tone. One of Mom's recommendations for coping was to stay connected or to reconnect with our children. In her counseling practice, she heard the pain associated with the loss of connections with adult children. She emphasized that we need to maintain our relationships.

Another coping skill particularly as women is to nurture our sense of identity within relationships. Mom told the women that to make the most of our golden years, "We need to stand back and view ourselves as women who have a lot to offer—to our families, our friends, our children—with a vast repository of knowledge of family history and gracious wisdom."

Mom went on to share multiple ideas for continuing to provide useful service in the community through volunteering—working with children, visiting the sick and those confined to nursing homes—and keeping a sharp mind by learning something new and playing games. Mom and I shared a common sacred mission to consciously own our power and boldly empower others to transform through their emotional uncertainty.

This beautiful revelation deeply expresses the magic and miracles in our connection. To recognize after Mom's death that we shared mutual life values has been enlightening and profoundly transformative. Following the revelatory process of an inner spiritual relationship with ourselves and our loved ones leads us grow and empowers our own life' after their death.

She recommended a book called *Necessary Losses* by Judith Viorst, in which the author discusses the stages of life where various losses can occur. Viorst specifically notes that aging is also a loss—one that is often unacknowledged.

Loss comes in numerous forms, needing our attention throughout our lives. Several weeks after receiving the notes of Mom's speech, I happened to glance into the cabinet where many of her treasures are kept and surprisingly discovered this book, *Necessary Losses,* that I had inherited. This is perfect divine alignment!

Mom speaks of our dynamic energies, the creative magic within all of us, and the shared challenges we all face—being in limbo and a sense of worthlessness—and her antidote is to have something to do, someone to love, and something to anticipate.

She said that all of us can feel anxious at times. Anxiety feeds on anxiety, but energy builds on energy; we can choose which energy is our highest alignment and most purposeful vibration.

Maintaining our sense of identity and validating ourselves is an important part of healthy aging. So is affirming our value and worth. I am grateful that she discovered her worth and learned how to validate herself at this later stage in her life.

Although, I didn't experience her energy in this way, it wasn't for her lack of trying. Therein lies the challenge of timing and a child's readiness to hear a particular lesson.

Our children are on their own soul journeys that present unique lessons for them. It takes time to integrate such knowledge. To communicate our life learning to our children we need to have lived the experience and embodied deep spiritual wisdom and value. Then our actions match our words. Sharing the growth and value of my successes and failures with my children opens a clearer channel for them to receive what they need.

Now, over thirty years later, I'm profoundly touched by hearing Mom's timeless and progressive wisdom. Healing our patterns for a blessing involves exploring our family experiences, our perceptions, our myths, and our shortcomings and challenging them to establish our truths.

One piece of my family trauma was healed while discussing this book with my sister, Cathy. She validated my sense of betrayal and confusion during the time of my parents' divorce and the following years by acknowledging that I couldn't have completely absorbed or understood all that was happening at a young age. Mom thought one day I'd need to talk about my experience, suspected she might not be alive, and requested that Cathy be available when that time came. Although I'd been working on these issues for a long time, hearing this care and concern was tremendously comforting.

During the grief process, linking the current loss to previous losses, not only the absence of a person but the qualities they represent, offers us a deeper understanding about our emotional and spiritual pain. We often uncover hidden treasures within our families and awaken to a greater love for them and within ourselves. Incorporating new wisdom and living in alignment with our truth allows us to make our loved one's legacy a blessing for all of humanity.

Discovering Mom's presentation notes was incredibly timely, both for writing this book—drawing on her moxie and bringing mine forward—and for the tremendous spiritual shifts occurring on our planet right now.

Growing climate change fears, the worldwide coronavirus pandemic, and the political upheaval intensified the turbulent effects of loss and uncertainty on both our collective and individual psyches and spirits. These tumultuous shifts around the globe are calling on us to wake up, pay attention, and reassess our engagement and contribution within our relationships in all our encounters.

Chapter 9

A WORLD WITHOUT MY MOM

"Appreciate that the end is never the end, but instead, is a new beginning filled with awe and wonder."

—Chaplain Candi Wuhrman

On Thursday morning, Mom seemed to be comfortably sleeping, and all was quiet. Cheri and Cathy were headed to shower, and I decided to go upstairs to the family activity room to do a little yoga.

I'd just laid out my yoga mat to begin my practice when I heard my mom's voice inside my head saying, "Candi, I'm going now."

I froze for a second, startled, and then understood and accepted what was happening. I responded in my head, "Okay, Mom. Don't forget, you'll be able to talk to me." Knowing what I know about dying moms, I didn't feel like I needed to run downstairs to see for myself.

Not a moment later, the nurse popped into the room and told me I should come because my mom was getting close.

I quickly ran down the hall to the bathroom to tell Cathy and dashed down the stairs. I looked for Cheri, but she'd already made it to Mom's room and witnessed her last breath. I joined her at the bedside.

Mothers often die when no one is around. I'm told they don't want their kids—even adult children—to see them die. I've deciphered with many of my patients and families that a mother leaving her children is already tremendously painful, and the thought of them watching her die might be even more stressful to her soul.

During our mom's dying process, we'd all gone to other areas of the house. When Cheri returned to Mom's room, she was in the involuntary process of taking her last breaths. Cheri described seeing her in her last moments as weird. Mom was already on her way, and those last gasps of breath were the energy that pushes the soul out of the body—birthing the soul—to go on its journey.

For many years, I wondered how I'd feel when my mom died. That day had come; was okay and in complete amazement…in awe. To do for my mom what I'd done for so many patients was beautiful. As her daughter, not her chaplain, I got to ask about her wishes, discuss death and dying, and fulfill her needs. It felt incredible to ease her way and honor her sacred end-of-life journey.

Of course, I felt sad, but not devastated. The hospice team and the mortuary were called, and we gathered up our things and packed up the car.

When the mortuary came and prepared to transport Mom, my sisters and I noticed a beautiful heavenly glow on Mom's face. As the mortuary attendants escorted Mom out, the hospice house caregivers lined the hallway and entryway to offer her a loving send-off. Mom would have loved that, and I was touched by their care.

Cathy and I drove off together to meet Cheri and my nieces at Mom's favorite burger place, and I burst into tears. The reality of Mom's death was hitting me, and I suddenly began to feel the effect of the entire energetic process of the last several days. I couldn't even go inside; I just needed to cry.

Death is a process, not an event. Connecting the two words, death and dying, often seems odd to most, but in the world of hospice and chaplaincy, they go hand-in-hand, and yet, are very different. Death is the finality of the body, ending life as we've known it, whereas dying is the journey of completing one's death—the dying process.

In a discussion entitled "Death: Process or Event?" between scholars Robert Morison and Leon Kass, they revealed a confusing inaccuracy by using the images of death and dying interchangeably. Our physical body is the vessel that exists only because of our soul's light. Death is the moment our life force ceases to animate our body. Dying is the process of natural aging and changing of the physical body so that at some point it can no longer house the soul—our breath of life. In this divine and sacred process, the soul organically transitions into the heavenly realm. Moxie is an expression of the life force within each of us.

I never would've known when I began authoring this spiritual journey that *Moxie* would take on a life of her own. My mom's enthusiasm was her flow of divine presence. I never saw her energetic expressions as godly, and in fact, questioned her intentions for a long time. I now believe that her divinely inspired force of nature was mysteriously present to encourage me to recognize my aspirations and inspirations for my own life's endeavors.

From a spiritual perspective, we are a soul within a body for a specific period of time. When we're born into our bodies, we are unaware of the life events we'll encounter or why. This is the human journey.

According to Jewish mystical practices, the Kabbalistic Tree of Life lives within each person. The Tree's roots, trunk, and branches correspond to the body and house the mechanisms for the soul's spiritual evolution. The Hebrew word Kabbalah is defined as "receiving." We embody divine attributes that connect and guide our emotional, instinctual, and intellectual life energy.

This sacred journey that occurs within our beings is the energy of God endlessly working with us—creating and renewing our life force through our life experiences.

Divine emanations within the Tree of Life—wisdom, understanding, loving-kindness, strength, beauty, and splendor (to name a few)—align with the human body, holding rich multidimensional meanings. These vibrant energies reside within us in our moxie —a sacred force and source beyond our imagination.

Our Tree of Life is rooted in our ancestry and heritage. It is connected to the Earth and the heavenly realms. These ties are often unexplainable, unseen, and untouchable energies that truly exist. Recognizing this internal guidance system affirms that a holy presence is guiding us in ethical and moral matters. This spiritual practice is organically designed to help us think through processes, wrestle through challenges, resolve issues, and receive solutions. Our job is to simply connect with that source of energy.

Our sacred moxie energy is speaking to us constantly. She calls on us to process our daily life experiences so that we can live our most vibrant lives. Living life to the fullest means we strive to create, dance, grow, and sing; Moxie says, "Feel and connect with it all." This internal force is powerfully knocking on the door of our spiritual house, asking us to connect, engage, and explore to evolve and transform our souls.

One day, after listening to the song "A Thousand Years" for the umpteenth time, I heard deep within my soul my mom's spirit telling me that she has loved me for a thousand years and will love me for a thousand more. I realized this was my mom's unconditional, endless love. I had heard her say she loved me so many times in my life and never felt it as powerfully as I do now. *Why, after she died, am I getting this intense message of love? What was she telling me and just what did this mean?* I had to explore even deeper. As I kept listening and crying, I continued to receive more messages.

The energy of this love can only be described as divine—a holy presence that surpasses all else. I'm not suggesting my mom was God. However, this indescribable energetic presence felt sacred and powerful beyond measure—a timeless uncondition al love like how I feel with my Creator.

This spiritual experience (and I've had many) was different—profoundly unique, fully-enveloping—a presence of infinite love I'd never known.

Mom's ambition and persistent nudging seemed very different. I finally understood her overly enthusiastic nature as was, in all her innate divine expression. Prior to revelation, her words felt pushy and demanding, and now I experienced her as direct and straight- forward with warmth and grace beside me. It was a dramatic, enlightening shift in my perception of her.

I'd heard "unconditional love" but often felt that love was conditional. Even though I knew I was loved, I felt I needed to do the right thing to be loved. This beautiful, loving awareness created a bridge to my mom for me to receive her spirit's messages. Feeling into, getting to know, connecting, and trusting this energy built a new pathway for an ongoing relationship with my mom's soul.

My mom called me "Darling" at times, mostly when sending me special cards like "My Darling Candy-Andy." Cheesy, I know, but endearing.

Hearing "Darling" in the song and the directive to not be afraid was the beginning of finding my bravery again—finding strength in this horrifically painful journey of loss—and unearthing the gems awaiting me. The song's lyrics spoke directly to me, affirming my sense that I would find her and myself again.

The grief journey would change and transform me. She had faith in me and I now knew she could connect with me from the other side. In my deepest, darkest times, this sentiment gave me faith to go through the layers of my pain and uncertainty. As listened daily to the power and strength of these lyrics, my body and spirit shifted. My doubt began to fade away.

This song told me I wasn't alone and would never be as my new-found moxie was calling me to be brave and to love more even in the hardest and scariest moments.

Upon reflection, I'm profoundly awed by my own awakening and growth through my grief. What began as learning to live life without mom transformed into a beautiful garden rich with deep awareness, divine connection, expansion, and enlightenme nt beyond what I could've imagined.

My discoveries were painful, not unlike breaking apart the layers of an onion with tears streaming down my face. Then shifting into a little sweeter process gently pulling the soft petals of a flowering artichoke, mindful of the prickly ends, tasting each morsel, and removing the protective layer to embrace the tender heart. Traveling the inner landscape of the soul is a delicate and sacred journey.

Sometimes the mess *is* the message. I began to see a glimmer of this awakening during the first Jewish holiday, Passover, following the death of my mom. I thought it would be a great idea to be with family on one of the first big occasions after her death, so I planned for my husband and I to be with my cousin for a *seder*, (meaning "order"), the ritual meal where the Passover story is told. However, my husband became ill, so we declined the invitation.

Initially, disappointed for needing to cancel, I reached out to my sisters, Cheri, for the recipe for Mom's chopped liver (the only one I ever liked). This opened conversation and created a new connection with my sister which had been challenging since Mom's death. I then set a seder table with a mishmash of dishes and all the family pictures to make an incomplete but meaningful seder.

My mom would've been horrified.
None of the dishes, silverware,
or glasses matched on my table, yet this is
the messiness and disorder I felt inside.
The energy of moxie inspired me every step of the way.
It was a perfect experience representing my mournful inner
landscape—surprisingly comforting, honoring Mom and my
whole family—which became a blessing.

Honoring a dear one's memory may involve making a heartfelt contribution, such as a financial gift or developing a project. While these contributions to honor a legacy are beautiful, the blessing might come from bringing a deeply buried painful truth to the forefront, which can also honor your loved one by healing an issue they were unable to address. Courageously facing the challenge and speaking out can bless us with freedom and sanctify our planet.

In my mind, stating, "May their memory be for a blessing" for the mourners as our communities gather after a loss, means more than a financial contribution. Our monetary contributions honor our loved ones and help organizations thrive. However, after many years, I've determined that this sentiment challenges us to explore our memories and glean the gems of wisdom from the relationship. We mine their imprints within our hearts and souls. This brings their legacy alive in our own lives. This is precisely the meaning of carrying the torch—that roaring fire of our loved one's divine essence—forward in the world. We nourish the seeds they've planted and nurture the design of their garden. Often, our planted seeds hold similar hopes of growing deep roots and flourishing with abundant beauty. We simply pick up where they left off. Gardening requires us to prune as we grow, discovering colorful hidden buds. The same is true within our divine inner garden. Sometimes, under the rocks, debris, and thorns, beyond the mess, we unearth sparks of a more authentic part of ourselves.

For me, connecting with my mom's love in my grief made me realize the divine gifts that I'd only just begun to bring into the world. I recognize that my awareness is what the world needs now and that honoring my inner calling, starting a private chaplaincy practice, writing a book, embracing my creativity, and increasing my visibility on social networks are my bold moxie needing to be expressed. It's time to take risks, be different, and be me because I love the me I've become.

It doesn't matter if others already think you are out there because you are already out there more than they are. What matters is that you are out there as much as you want to be or are called to be.

The pain of holding back became greater than the fear of moving forward. Within the deepest, darkest abyss searching for my mom, I discovered an immeasurab le love. This mystical, mysterious, unexplainab le divine love reaches beyond measures and boundaries with all humanity which has inspired me to be a channel for love within our world.

Do we shrink ourselves and recoil from being more visible and vulnerable in the world?

When I look back at Mom's life—how much she loved dancing and live performances—I realize those activities enlivened her spirit. Mom was a phenomenal dancer and taught in her adult years. I'd heard inklings of her past desire to open a dance studio.

While writing *Moxie*, I became aware that her dream was squelched by the times and expectations in the 1950s and 60s. Women were expected to remain in the home, and although may have felt an inner calling to express themselves, the all-too-common patterns of shrinking back and putting their man's needs and work-life first were prevalent.

I clarified this awareness with my sister Cathy. Although I'm the youngest in our family and wasn't privy to the specific details of most situations, I had a sense of my mom's lost dream and the squelching of her divine energy.

Cathy told me that Mom wanted to teach dance. However, at the same time Dad gave her his permission, he also imposed a stipulation that Mom could teach dance lessons as long as dinner was on the table by six o'clock each evening. During these less-than-progressive times, I suspect my mom must've felt teaching would've caused an upheaval to the family household.

Further contemplating my relationship with Mom, and now embracing my creativity more, I wondered if Mom's nudges were the unexpresse d creative energy of *her* unfulfilleddream to teach dance.

One Sukkot, my favorite Jewish holiday, while sitting in my *sukkah* (a shelter), a hummingbird flew right into my sacred space. Wings humming, she stared directly at me. My thoughts quickly went to Mom.

"Are you here?" I asked.

She didn't respond directly. However, a Hebrew prayer came to mind with the words translated as "...spread over us your shelter of peace..." This was particularly poignant because it came while sitting in my sukkah. The combination of these three things, the sukkah, the hummingbird, and the prayer, assured me that Divine Mystery is ever-present. I experienced a profound sense of connection that my mom, my dad, and all my ancestors were energetically supporting me. Together, they reminded me to trust Spirit's presence, protection, and peace. These types of occurrences get our attention and bring reassurance in uniquely specific ways and awaken us to the Divine within and all around us.

Our lives and all within them are impermanent. We face uncertainty and transition constantly. Relationships change continuously. Our children grow up, move out, and create families of their own. Our loved ones die, and new little ones arrive. Friendships change. Everything evolves as we grow, move, and shift within our consciousness. Life is fragile, but our spirits are vibrant. We all crave balance, equanimity, and peace and can create our own internal and external sacred places.

These sacred structures are built with the energy of our relationships with our families, friends, communities, and Divine Presence, providing us with a sense of belonging, connection, and wholeness. Recognizing these sacred moments in our daily practices enlightens and enriches our physical lives and blesses us with peace. The strength and stability of these bonds flows out into our personal and professional lives, in our various communities and groups, and across the world.

Unfolding the endless layers of grief offered me the gift of seeing my mom and dad in different ways—they were two powerful forces in the world.

My mom didn't share her growth challenges with me. I'm guessing she didn't want to burden me.

As a mom, I've been the same with my children. We're supposed to be the strong ones, right?

Although Mom authentically and vulnerably shared her emotions, I didn't know what steps she took to grow from her experiences. She influenced me by sheer presence. However, I didn't learn her methods of human and spiritual development—her practices, tools, and tricks—until much later. I'm certain I absorbed wisdom from her along the way. Again, one's internal growth processes and emotional expressions weren't discussed in those times and were even seen as weaknesses.

My dad hid his vulnerabilities, at least from me, but I now see his rough edges as a means of charging forward to strengthen the path for our family. If he'd let his trials disempower him, he would never have created a better life for himself and ultimately for us.

I wish my childhood had been different, but that's just how it happened. Mom and Dad's choices presented challenging examples for me at times with a lot to work through. Yet, many years later, I began to see—and then genuinely appreciate—their acts of bold moxie and their vibrance for life as deeply rooted values. I internalized both qualities, and they unknowingly became gifts I passed on to my children by example. Although life still presents me with opportunities for healing, I now recognize the blessings woven into my parents' legacy.

Over the years, I often wondered if Mom believed in God. The name rarely crossed her lips. Dad never mentioned spiritual connection either. Yet we were rooted in Jewish life—we belonged to synagogue communities , celebrated holidays, and participated in religious school. While we didn't speak openly about divinity, I've come to believe they both felt a sacred energy—something mysterious and holy— that lived through their courage, creativity, and vibrant presence. That sacred life force was moxie. It's a divine thread of powerful energy that flows through our family line. We all carry it. We've inherited it. And we pass it on.

Grief, I've learned, is one of the ways this energy awakens.

To transform through grief is to reconnect with what we believe we've lost—including parts of ourselves. The people we love make an imprint on our souls, and when they die, it can feel like a piece of us is missing too. But if we're willing to enter that aching space with curiosity and courage, we may discover it's also a doorway—one that leads us deeper into our own becoming. Within that hollow space, wisdom arises. The soul speaks. And we remember: the heart's deepest connections remain intact, because spirit never dies.

For me, the grief experience—the depths of emotion—is devastatingly painful. But embracing the endless tidal waves of sadness and sorrow feels like it was given me for a purpose. I came to see each crest, each swell of ache, as an opportunity. Her absence—and strangely, her presence—met me in those waves, inviting me into energetic connection. As I reached out to her, lamenting, longing, and desperately missing , something shifted. The grief became a bridge. A passage. I guided me into deeper understanding and meaning. And in that space, I experienced what I knew was always possible: *her spirit was profoundly still with me.*

My mom's love didn't end with her death. In fact, I became more aware of her love through the process of grieving. Grief makes room for a different kind of knowing. Divine love—that infinite, sacred energy line—is what continues to connect us, beyond time and beyond form. Death doesn't undo love. What changes is the way our loved ones express their love.

The magic and mystery of grief lies in its capacity to transform us. When we surrender to its currents, we're drawn into a larger, unseen reality. Grief opens us. It tears down the walls that once protected us from feeling, and through that rupture, we are made ready. Ready to encounter Spirit. Ready to glimpse the spiritual realm in ways we may never have known before.

Before my mom died, I knew I would grieve. That part was certain. But I had no idea what sacred encounters would come through that grief. I expected pain, the aching emptiness of her absence. And yes, that came. But what I hadn't anticipated was the sacredness of the hollow space itself. I had to travel through it to find what was waiting. Those hollow spaces became hallowed spaces. Not just voids, but vessels. Sacred containers for the transformation of my heart and soul.

When a person is in the dying process, they exist between two realms—the physical and the spiritual. They're leaving behind their tangible, touchable form and becoming pure soul essence. We, too, transition. In our grief, as we slowly recalibrate our lives, we begin to reflect on our relationship with them—not just who they were, but how they impacted us. Grief then becomes more than sorrow. It becomes a sacred threshold where transformation begins to move us forward.

There is a spiritual realm that lives beyond our imagination—some feel it as a physical place, others as energy. It may be a sense of heaven, nirvana, a spirit world. Some experience it as union with God, Divine Presence, Source, or simply the Great Mystery. Whatever name resonates for you, this realm is not confined to doctrine. It is infinite, often nameless. It moves through the whirling wind, the shining sun, the swaying trees, and the whispering silence. Source Energy beats in our hearts, flows within every breath, and holds us in our most human moments. It is the energy of connection, and it never dies.

Grief is not something to be endured—it is something to be experienced. No one can tell us how to grieve. Each journey is unique. The very word emotion speaks to its nature: energy in motion. Grief asks everything of us, but offers us an opportunity to flourish. When we draw on our moxie in the midst of grief, we gain the courage to feel fully, to learn openly, and to embrace a softening of our hearts. This is a force—greater than us and within us—guiding us gently home to ourselves.

Sitting still, thinking of Mom, I feel her lively, energetic presence: her excitement about blooming flowers, changing seasons, music, and dance. Even with her appreciation for life, she was occasionally pierced by the thorns on the stems of her roses and even missed a step now and again.

Disappointment, pain, and sorrow are real parts of lifeand need to be felt. When life gets tough, and it will, we search deeply within our heart and soul for strength and inspiration. Moxie, our inner fire, leads us to ask to bigger questions, *Who am I now?* and *What's next?*

Howard Thurman, an American author and known mystic, said, "Don't ask yourself what the world needs. Ask yourself what makes you come alive, and go do that, because what the world needs are people who have come alive." This timeless wisdom and profound vision are the epitome of moxie magic. Our aliveness is our moxie. That spitfire that awakens from deep within calls us face tough things to grow and rise higher. It's all mysterious and miraculous.

I still miss my mom, but I know she's with me. Sometimes it feels like she never left. I smile when I recall her joy in seeing the grandchildren, hearing about my cooking, or playing cards together. I often feel the energy of Mom clapping her hands and dancing to her music.

Mom embodied a divine presence—communicated through her enthusiasm, inspiration, and vibrance. I didn't always see her that way, but since her death, I do. Mom's zest for life taught me that there is something magical in every day, within every person, and that love is always present, even when we can't see or feel it. The energy of love is immeasurable and unending.

When we awaken to the truth that life is hard—and still choose to live fully through our difficulties—beautiful adventures begin to unfold. So, play the hand you're dealt. Cry the tears that need to flow, and listen to what they're teaching you. We grieve so deeply and feel the depth of loss because our souls are connected, and we've loved so greatly.

Spiritual transformation and mystical connection is available to everyone. It calls on us to grow and change. Denying trauma and trying to bypass the deeper inner work leaves our hearts heavy and our spirits stifled. You and your family deserve courageous and sacred conversatio ns. Heal the hurt that hardens your heart, squelches your voice, and blocks your light. A joyful life and a graceful death depend on it.

The sacred rhythm of music and dance connects us to the energy of our own Divine Spirit. This journey is about seeking that connection again and again. Like my mom's fierce enthusiasm, sacred inspiration often arrives in surprising ways—wrapped in the ordinary, but hiding in plain sight.

The Source of Life's energy is already inside of you. When waves of grief pull you under, surrender to them. Slide into the tunnel, ride the swells, and rise with it until the light of the sun greets you again. Like a skilled surfer, you will learn to ride the ebb and flow of the emotional tides. Look for the ways this sacred journey brings blessings of enlightenme nt and inspiration.

Find the spirit of moxie that awakens and illuminates your magic, miracles, and mystery throughout your life. Carry the torch of radiant light that has been passed to you across generations. Embrace every flicker of the flame for all that it has to teach you. Dance the rhythm in your heart. Trust that your children—and their children—will share your legacy in ways that aligns with their spirit.

Ponder the existential meanings of life and discover why you exist. Live the questions, because the answers will change as you evolve. Appreciate that the end is never the end, but instead, a new beginning filled with awe and wonder.

May your grief journey propel you forward into the most amazing spiritual transformation, and may you live vibrantly with the blessings of *Moxie.*

BEING RESOURCEFUL

Being ReSourceful means doing the sacred work of connecting with your inner truth—returning to your SELF: Source Energy Loving Force—and finding your Source. My intention is to encourage, empower, and guide you toward the right resources that resonate with your unique healing needs. A familiar quote from The Talmud reminds us, "When you give a man a fish, you feed him for a day. When you teach a man to fish, you feed him for a lifetime."

Tuning into your inner alignment will lead you in the most life-affirming direction. Alignment elevates your self-esteem, strengthens your connection with your soul, and builds trust within. Following your unfolding path cultivates resilience and nurtures your faith to step into your next adventure.

There are many valuable avenues for individual and group experiences. I'e explored several paths throughout my process of discovery, healing, and spiritual growth. Each professional brings their own essence—their personality, skillset, style, and values. While I can only endorse resources I've personally experienced, I'd be honored to help you discern what resonates for you.

After a loss, friendships and other relationships change. It's important to create a nourishing support circle with people who feel aligned with where you are now. I call my sacred circle a "God squad"—the people who know me deeply, love me uncondition ally, and understand me without much explanation. These relationships take time to build. We're not always emotionally in the same place, and that's okay. My circle has evolved as I've grown, revealing new needs and new desires. Sometimes, we outgrown people or they outgrow us. It's not a failure—it's evolution.

While there are many resources out there, the greatest truth I've found is that the healing journey is about being present with and process all that surfaces. Transformation takes time. Grief is an organic process of life—and often, the most complex, confusing, and misunderstood set of experiences. I can't take away your grief, and I wouldn't because the pain and journey have purpose But I *can* walk you through it. That's my sacred work—guiding clients, patients, and families through the terrain grief transformation.

I may not be your person—but will help you find who is. If there were a magic pill, I'd offer it. But the true magic lives in the journey itself—the slow, sacred process of your alignment. Within your grief lives mystical moxie. Within the ache are the hidden gems that will light up your life, your soul, and your relationships. To further explore the topics of death, dying, grief, loss, and trauma, visit: http://www.sacredworkwithcandi.com.

I'm honored to guide you in finding the right path for you. Through my concierge chaplaincy practice, I offer programming and support for individuals, couples, and entire families—facing end-of-life, grief healing, spiritual process work, and the kind of deep transformation that comes from addressing longstanding spiritual injuries.

As I often say: ***"Spiritual injuries occur when traumatic events hurt our spirit and unknowingly cause us to ignore our voice, forget our joy, and hide our light."*** — Chaplain Candi Wuhrman

I'd be deeply honored to accompany you through your grief and the sacred awakenings that await you.

With Love and Light,

Chaplain Candi

GLOSSARY

Adverse childhood experiences (ACEs)—the events that occur in the early years of life and affect people's health and well-being not only at the time of the event but also later in life.

B'tzelem Eloheim—the Hebrew words meaning that one is created in the image or likeness of God.

Chai—the Hebrew word for Life.

Chesed—the Hebrew word for loving-kindness.

Chochmah—the Hebrew word for wisdom.

Crossover—a term used for when a person dies and crosses over from the physical world into the spiritual realm.

Divine Presence—a presence or sensation of a holy sacred existence; something beyond human; a sense of godliness; a profound sense of awe; may be related to a religious practice or belief; a greater awareness of spirituality, felt within; around the human being, and engaging with others.

Ego—a person's sense of self-esteem or self-importance; the "I" or self of any person.

For a blessing—*"May their memory be for a blessing"*—a customary Jewish statement of comfort and honor offered to the mourner after the death of a loved one; holding the greater meaning of bringing something of the deceased loved one's legacy to the world; sharing wisdom gleaned by being in relationship with that person.

God—Source of the Universe, a deity, a common name used to identify a supreme being, can be an all-encompassing name for the Source of Creation and Divine Presence.

Hashem—the Hebrew word meaning *The Name*, which is used in place of specific names such as God for the Divine.

Intensive—extensive programming that creates focused healing in a shorter concentrated time frame; very thorough or vigorous.

Kabbalah—the Hebrew word meaning *"receiving*;" an esoteric discipline of Jewish Mysticism that reveals many qualities of Divine Presence within the soul-body construct; the relationship of *sefirot* (emanations) within the human being explains how the person processes divine awareness and wrestles with life struggles.

Kaddish—a specific prayer for mourners. In traditional Jewish observance, a child recites the mourners' *kaddish* daily for an entire year after a parent dies, on each anniversary (*Yahrzeit),* and many of the Jewish holidays thereafter. Individual family members recite *kaddish* for different lengths of time.

Life Force—the internal power or inspiration that gives something its vibrance, vitality, or strength; the spirit or energy that animates the human being; the soul.

Netzach—the seventh of ten emanations of God within the Jewish mystical system of *Kabbalah* means eternity, endurance, and victory.

Passover—In Hebrew, *Pesach*. In Judaism, the holiday commemorates the Exodus of the Israelites from slavery in Egypt; the "passing over" the houses of the Israelites, sparing their firstborn.

Seder—Hebrew word meaning order; a Jewish ritual service and ceremonial dinner for the first two nights of Passover.

Shechinah—the Hebrew meaning "*God's dwelling* or *presence*;" the feminine aspect of the Divine embodying attributes such as love and compassion; often symbolizing a sheltering cloud or a pillar of fire.

Shiva—a Jewish practice providing a seven day period to begin the time of mourning for the deceased, beginning immediately after the funeral; a mourner *sits shiva*.

Soul—the spiritual or immaterial part of a human being; human life force that animates our physical structure and provides an inseparable connection to our Creator.

Source—an entity, a place, or an origination of something or someone; a free-flowing energy presence that can be embraced or obtained.

Spirit—an intangible presence of the holy and sacred that is similar to other names for God, Divine Presence, or Source; a nonphysical energetic vibrational force that guides the human being.

Spirit-to-Spirit Conversations—a facilitated process of communication between two entities—one alive seeking information, the other deceased or not present—to bring understanding to a relationship: soul-to-soul energetic conversation.

Spiritual Injuries—occur when traumatic events hurt our spirit and unknowingly cause us to ignore our voice, forget our joy, and hide our light.

Sukkah—a temporary shelter built for the Jewish holiday of Sukkot; many observe the holiday by dwelling, eating meals, and sharing with guests in the *sukkah* for 7 days.

Sukkot—one of the three harvest holidays expressing gratitude and joy for God's provisions.

Talmud—Hebrew word for study or learning. The central text of Rabbinic Judaism and the primary source of Jewish religious law and Jewish theology.

ACKNOWLEDGMENTS

My heartfelt gratitude and appreciation goes to:

- My God, Spirit, and Divine Energy—the Oneness that has channeled through every word.
- My mom, my dad, and all my ancestors for divinely inspiring me, for their spiritual presence, and the profound energetic messages that have called and propelled me forward to commit to this huge endeavor.
- My beloved husband, Arnie, for patiently waiting for this incredible endeavor to come to fruition and his undying faith in me.
- My children, Michelle and Josh, for believing in me, cheering me on, and allowing me to share our lived experiences.
- My sister Cathy, who has always been there for me, for being interested throughout this journey, discovering our mom's note-cards, listening to the unfolding layers of my childhood grief, and offering insight.
- My sister Cheri, who has been there for me, shares her grand-kids with me, for being open to me writing about her, sharing

our life experiences with our mom, and for rich conversations revealing secrets and building deeper connections.

- My dear friend and soul sister Katja, who has always been eager to read anything I've ever written, even edited my grad school papers, taught me to be a better writer, has always supported my spiritual journey, and showed up for the joys and pains of my book's unfolding. I even entrusted this book to Katja during the process if anything happened to me to ensure its completion and publication.
- All of my beloved family and friends who have cheered me on, encouraged me, and loved me along this divinely creative journey.
- All of my colleagues and teachers over my many years of study.
- A sincerest thank you goes to my dear friend, writing mentor, and editing partner, LoisAnne. She is a writing teacher and a published author. LoisAnne's meticulous grammar and excellent vocabulary made exploring word meanings and subject matter a pleasure. As I read my manuscript aloud to her, we shared many humorous moments. We were two moxie spirits partnering together who brought our highest divine selves for the greater good. Hearing, seeing, and feeling LoisAnne's response to my writing provided immeasurable feedback, a critical eye to examine my writing flow, and encouragement that let me know that my words and message would indeed make an impact. Working with LoisAnne has been like giving my book an early debut. Having the opportunity to share my heart and soul along the writing journey was a cathartic experience for me and gave more meaning and depth to my publication.
- Kristina Edstrom & Lexi Mohney for my gorgeous cover design.

PRAISE FOR MOXIE

Moxie is a book that comes directly from Candi's heart and soul. Reading Candi's book is very much like sharing a deeply intimate, spiritual journey with her. Anyone who has experienced grief will relate to this book. Candi is a brilliant chaplain, and her new book exemplifies it.

Chaplain Marlene Canter
Academy for Jewish Religion, California 2015

* * *

Reading *Moxie*, it becomes clear we are not alone on the grief journey as we move from mourning the loss to dancing with spirit. *Moxie* contains a roadmap for awakening into bolder versions of ourselves by letting go of what separates us from our inner truth. Having worked with Chaplain Candi and relied on her support after the death of my mother, I was inclined to trust Candi to be both direct and kind. As a hospice physician for fifteen years, I have often heard that we "can't fix the family" when speaking of the limitations inherent in our work with our patients and families.

I see in *Moxie* courageous, deeply spiritual examples of how grieving family members can heal, even "fix" broken relationships as they work through their grief. This is an excellent resource for those grieving and those working in the field of spiritual support around grief.

Dr. Kempe Ames
Medical Director

* * *

The book *Moxie* is a testament to the rich spiritual transformation that grief work provides. It holds a feisty energy but is delivered with gentle compassion and deep understanding from Chaplain Candi.

Chaplains are ministers in secular places. We have a great opportunity to touch the lives of every person we encounter, no matter what their background or creed. Chaplain Candi and the tenets of *Moxie* leave the reader longing to soothe the grief that comes from losing people and things that are special to us. Chaplain Candi is an empathic guide who will walk with you through all the feelings of grief with wisdom, skill, and kindness.

Countess Clarke Cooper, MBA, MDiv, STM
Military Chaplain, USAF DCNG
Founder of The Rainbow Nation CC
Author, Speaker, Coach, Entrepreneur
Author of *Ignite Your Spirit: 10 Steps to Transform Your Spirit and Embrace Your Amazing Self*

* * *

Moxie, an impressive memoir from Chaplain Candi Wuhrman, shares her own grief experiences with insight and wisdom. As she shares her experiences in deep grief, you can almost feel the "waves" as they hit her with emotions to process. Wuhrman describes the depth of pain and the feelings of awe that follow as she comes to understand the power of the love connecting her to her mother both before and after death. Her descriptions of breakthroughs in her processing show us there can be joy in the discovery of the love and the connectedness of the Divine.

Growing up and pondering adulthood, Wuhrman's mother kept pushing her to find her "moxie." It is evident Chaplain Candi has found her moxie in her career commitment as she teaches the reader about aspects of spiritual transitioning, death, and passing to the other side. In this exceptional book, Wuhrman has taken human emotions of grief and interprets them as holy pathways to the Divine.

Cathy A. Kass, Ed.D.
Retired Professor
Volunteer, Miller Hospice

* * *

In her book, *Moxie: A Hospice Chaplain's Journey Through Grief*, author Candi Wuhrman takes us with her as she tells her intimate and tender story of her journey of grief in losing her mom and finding her way on the spiritual path. She writes about the unraveling as she moved through her loss and the courage it takes to bring the aspects of life back together. She shares her spiritual practices and revelations with an open heart. I appreciated hearing about her inner processes and how they supported her outer transformation. I highly recommend Candi's book to anyone going through their own loss and grief.

Rev. Christine Green
Inspiring Conscious Evolution

* * *

Chaplain Wuhrman's book is a combination of reflective practice, storytelling, and wisdom for the ages and processes of grief.

Wuhrman shares a rich landscape of personal vulnerabilities to assist her readers in opening up divinity in all areas of life, including loss, grief, change, joy, and human triumph.

Moxie provides "steppingstones" into deepening relationships and internal wisdom. If there is any book that expertly and sensitively joins illumination and splendor with the profundity of loss, this is it.

Wuhrman's recipe for doing this is unique. *Moxie: A Hospice Chaplain's Journey through Grief* is full of courage, determination, and the kind of moxie that makes life richer and more transcendent.

Rabbi Rochelle Robins, ACPE Certified Educator
Ezzree Institute, President and Co-Founder

* * *

Candi's artful writing positions us in a sacred conversation with not only the text—from which we can learn, but also in a dialectic with our grief. She creates a gracious liminal space for us to sit in beginner's mind and view our suffering—not as a punishment or something to be endured—but as a birthright, blessing, and an abundant and verdant field that allows us to envision new vistas of being and individuation that we might not have experienced, had we not gone through the grief.

What I love most about Candi's writing is this concept of the animating principle of moxie—a who rather than a what—who lovingly walks us through our grief experiences. We are reminded that we are not alone…that our own form of moxie is with us.

From the personality she weaves into *Moxie* as animated by her darling mother to the well-crafted, albeit tough truths about grief that she weaves among the stories, sentences like:

"An illuminated path is tough to see when the pain is so great…"

"…death is a process, not an event…" (often that we must endure), and,

"…most of us hold our breath waiting for the pain of loss to pass…"

The beauty of her interfaith approach is gloriously inclusive and welcoming of all faith and spiritualist traditions, and it creates a fertile ground for us to invite psyche, soma, and spirit along in our own grief journeys. If you are navigating any grief, this book is a must-read.

Jenny Rain, Ph.D.
Founder of Jenny Rain Coaching

* * *

Extending beyond the confines of a memoir, *Moxie: A Hospice Chaplain's Journey Through Grief* by Chaplain Candi Wuhrman is a practical guide and spiritual compass for anyone navigating the intertwined paths of grief and end-of-life preparation. Among its many insights, the discussion on anticipatory grief profoundly resonated with me, illuminating the often-overlooked aspect of preparing the soul for what lies ahead.

As the oldest daughter of elderly parents, *Moxie* empowered me to approach delicate topics with confidence and grace. The insights provided by Chaplain Wuhrman have been invaluable, enabling me to ensure that my parents can face their final days with dignity and peace. It's rare to find a book that so effectively combines personal narrative with actionable advice, making *Moxie* a unique and essential resource.

Laura L. Zielke, MDiv, CC
Holistic Nonprofit Executive Coach

* * *

In *Moxie*, Candi weaves a heartfelt narrative that not only traverses the rugged terrain of grief but also illuminates the transformative power of enduring love. Through her intimate journey alongside her mother, she uncovers the multifaceted nature of grief—a journey that is as personal as it is universal. What strikes me most profoundly is how Candi frames grief not as a path to merely endure but as an opportunity for profound personal growth and spiritual awakening.

Her honest exploration into the depths of her own heartache serves as a beacon for anyone navigating the turbulent waters of losing a loved one. This book doesn't shy away from the complexities of the human spirit but instead embraces them, offering insights that resonate with the soul's capacity to heal and find meaning amidst loss.

Candi's narrative is a testament to the resilience of the human heart, offering steppingstones for those who find themselves lost in their grief. The concept of *Moxie's* Five Initiations presents a framework not just for surviving but thriving through the labyrinth of loss.

It's a narrative that empowers, heals, and transforms, guiding the reader toward a renewed sense of self and a deeper connection with the world around them.

As someone who has always believed in the power of personal transformation and the impact of sharing our truths, I find Candi's courage in telling her story not just admirable but deeply inspiring. *Moxie* is more than a book; it's a journey through the heart of grief, illuminated by the enduring light of love and the unbreakable spirit of the human soul. For anyone seeking comfort, understanding, or a way to honor their loved one's legacy, this book is a guiding star.

Kerstin Decook
Author / Speaker / Leadership Coach CPC/ELI-MP
Break Loose and Fly Coaching

ABOUT THE AUTHOR

CHAPLAIN CANDI WUHRMAN understands grief and is revolutionizing the path of healing across the globe. She is a Board-Certified Clinical Chaplain, longtime Hospice Chaplain, Spiritual Counselor, and Grief Transformation Coach and Guide. As a proud U.S. Army Veteran, Chaplain Candi holds a Masters in Spiritual Psychology, a Masters in Jewish Studies and Theology, and a Certificate in Jewish Chaplaincy. With over three decades of experience with transformational spiritual work for herself and with others, Candi has been with thousands of individuals and entire families at the end of life and throughout their grief journeys.

Candi is the Founder and CEO of Sacred Work with Candi, where she is changing the entire trajectory of the end-of-life experience and the grief process for generations to come. She recognizes that grief reveals and connects the many layers and threads within the woven tapestry of our lives. As a second-generation Holocaust survivor, Candi knows the elusive complexities of inherited imprints that affect our families and the course of grief. Having experienced childhood losses, she has embraced her pain and discovered the sacred journey of spiritual connection and transformation. In her innovative programs, ReSOULution: Sacred Conversations and Connections From Diagnosis Through Grief, Death, and Beyond and Family Healing Intensives, Candi reconnects the heart and soul of the family, heals the intergenerational cultural and familial trauma, and profoundly changes lives at the core level.

In her work, Candi demonstrates a passion for walking alongside individuals in their spiritual evolution. She facilitates profound connection, integration, and transformation through communication challenges, illness diagnoses, the dying experience, the grief journey, and trauma resolution. Candi finds great comfort and joy in knowing that facing our pain and processing our losses within relationships offers us an empowered path to heal the heart and soul and achieve emotional balance for a lifetime.

Candi lives amidst the gorgeous Oregon trees with her husband, Arnie. Together they have two thriving adult children, Michelle and Josh. Candi loves hiking in the woods, kayaking and swimming in the Willamette River, and nurturing her flowers.

Chaplain Candi's sacred purpose is transforming the grief experience—resolving inner turmoil and healing the spirit—which in turn connects each soul with their divine light and the blessed memory of their loved one's.

Visit https://www.sacredworkwithcandi.com

JUST ANOTHER BEGINNING

No end, just another bold and courageous step forward. Through the painful moments of grief, remember that there is a whole new realm of experience that's awakening and guiding you. Feel the music that connects you to your rhythm. Find the movement that feels right for you. Grief is an array of experiences filled with a plethora of emotions, a journey to be felt.

Here's a picture of me with my mom taken in 2013. I gave it to her expressing my thanks and appreciation. After she died, I got it back. Now, this photo sits on my desk and beautifully invites my mom to be with me.

Will You Post a Review at Your Favorite Retailer?
If you've been touched by what you've read in *Moxie: A Hospice Chaplain's Journey Through Grief*, please post an honest review. My book is available at Amazon.com, Barnes & Noble, and through all your favorite bookstores. This will help me reach more people with this message. Thank You!

With Gratitude and Appreciation
If this book has added a little more comfort, ease, understanding, or wisdom to meet your grief, your family, and your spiritual evolution through pain—would you help me pass the magic, message, and mystery on?

Whether you're feeling more grounded, hopeful, and trusting with those who may be facing end of life and with the many unfolding aspects of the grief journey, I'd be so grateful if you shared the ways you've been touched.

A brief, honest review on Amazon (or wherever you picked up this book!) helps other individuals and their families find their unique pathway through accumulated grief and opens the door to healing, hope, and reSOULution—and helps to bring more peace and harmony to the world.

If you think five stars are earned, I'd be extra grateful.

Just scan this QR code here:

Made in the USA
Las Vegas, NV
02 December 2025

35603620R00121